Murder in Rural Hill

The Tragic Tale of Miss Janie Sharp
and Swinton Permenter

W. W. McCully

W.W. McCully

ISBN:
ISBN-13: 978-0692763735
(W.W. McCully)
ISBN-10: 0692763732

Dedicated to my wife, Tracy and my daughter, Myrrah
for their support and the freedom to pursue my
sometimes self-indulgent but always interesting pursuits.

"Sleep On, Dear Janie, Thy Work is Done

Thy Mortal Pangs are O'er

Jesus Has Come And Borne Thee Home

Beyond This World Of Sin And Woe"

CONTENTS

PREFACE

It was a typical hot, oppressive Sunday afternoon in July 2010. The dust from the gravel road hung in the air and coated the leaves of the nearby oaks as a small crowd gathered in a rural Methodist church in western Winston County, Mississippi. Some were returning to the same church where they had just attended services only a few hours before. Others were visiting this 150-year-old structure for the first time or at least the first time in many years.

This gathering was not a religious service, a reunion or a church business meeting. It was an acknowledgement of an anniversary of an event that occurred 100 years before; a horrific event that took the life of a vibrant young woman, ultimately led to the murder of at least two other individuals and destroyed the lives of several more including a young man accused of the murder. The events of July 21, 1910 impacted and shaped a community throughout the twentieth century.

I was always curious about the case of Janie Sharp. I knew little about her death as a child growing up in another part of the county but had since heard many fantastic versions but few true details.

This is a story that many did not want told and for many years, public discussion was discouraged. The families involved maintained deep ties and roots in the area. Feelings were strong and the unresolved nature of the case led to speculation and speculation led to conflict between kin and even between husbands and wives.

In my research, at least one party spoke of his grandparents, people who toiled and worked the land together, raised children, served God and their community, people who had few cross words in their marriage except about the guilt or innocence of a young man accused of a long ago murder.

Until the late 1970's, students at the local schools were forbidden to write essays or promote discussion about the case by the district superintendent for fear of opening old wounds.

The conflict, the loosely imposed censorship and the unresolved mystery kept the story of Janie Sharp alive. It was passed across kitchen tables and across quilt stands at sewing parties. It surfaced on front porches on Sunday afternoons, underneath shade trees, around feed store counters and country store gas pumps or anywhere that old men gathered.

Over the years, the facts have become unclear, encased in legend and subject to the desire to make a good story even more fantastic.

The murder of a young Janie Sharp and the ensuing trials and murders made national headlines, split a community for the better part of the 20th century and produced one of the most celebrated court cases in Mississippi history. Publicly, her murder and those of the others remain unresolved to this day.

INTRODUCTION

To tell the tale of a 106-year-old murder case is without question – a challenge. No one remains with firsthand knowledge of events and unfortunately, legal records are almost non-existent. Much of the direct information related to the events detailed here come from newspaper reports; reports that often contradict, exaggerate and without a doubt, contain inaccurate information. Sorting through the various news stories and conversations passed down from generation to generation, reviewing timelines, spellings and extracting truth from embellishment was a significant task.

The lack of information often resulted in gaps in timelines and a lack of understanding of motivations of principal characters. The temptation to speculate on events and make assumptions related to parts of this story was great. But I quickly realized that this would take more away from the tale than could possibly be gained. After all, this was an unsolved murder. In fact, there were three unsolved murders to be considered.

Everyone loves a good mystery and the case of Janie Sharp has remained a mystery for over 100 years. The lack of resolution of these events presents a rare challenge for the reader, an opportunity to examine the evidence, discuss, debate and to draw their own conclusions without undue influence upon the part of this writer.

****

It was Halloween. The previous week had been filled with hayrides, school carnivals, children (and sometimes adults) in silly or macabre costumes and giant bags of bite size candy. It was a time of fun but it was also a time of dread for those in positions of responsibility for Center Ridge Methodist Church.

Directly across a dusty rural gravel road lay the remains of Perninah Jane (Janie) Sharp. Her tombstone is easily identifiable, a tall marble obelisk located by the roadside behind a chain link fence that surrounds several acres of near ancient markers inscribed with familiar family names.

Over the years, to visit the grave of Janie Sharp had become a rite of passage for most high school students in the county. Ghost stories were rampant and the most prominent was that Janie would rise from the grave on Halloween night and search for her killer or that upon seeing Janie on the side of the road, you must stop and give her a ride or suffer the consequences of a deadly accident on your way home.

 While church members didn't mind the stories or the teenage visitors, the litter, beer cans and vandalism were another matter. In an effort to curtail these problems, church members held their own event, passing out candy to the little ones and gathering around a bonfire in the church yard in hopes of modifying the behavior of those who found the need to exhibit their bravery in confrontation with the ghost of a long dead teenage girl.

Sitting around that fire, I watched as wave after wave of teenagers and adults arrived by the carload in hopes of catching a glimpse of Janie; something – anything to make their heart pound, to get that adrenalin rush, to tell their friends about in school on Monday. Cell phone cameras flashed to capture images of a tombstone but more often than not – to capture images of themselves on a great adventure.

As I watched, I also listened to the conflicting tales told around that fire:

- *She was found in her wedding dress.*
- *No – she was carrying her wedding dress because she was on her way to have it altered.*
- *She was found hanging in a tree, a noose around her neck.*
- *No – she was hanging in a tree alright - not by a noose but by her long blonde hair.*
- *She was killed by a spurned lover.*

I quickly realized that the real story, the human story was lost in the legends. As the years since 1910 unfolded, the story grew bigger, more fantastic and convoluted until it became little more than a cautionary ghost tale to frighten children and make hearts race around a late evening campfire. The tales held little truth about Miss Janie and almost nothing was known about the tragedy of events after her death and the trials of young Swinton Permenter.

Over the years, the facts had become unclear, encased in legend and subject to the desire to make a good story even more fantastic. This book is an attempt to tell the story of Miss Janie, the young man accused of her murder and the ensuing aftermath in as straightforward a manner as possible.

In my research, I believe I discovered several things:

There were some underlying circumstances here that never made it to the surface. I won't speculate on those and the reader can form their own opinions.

The newspapers of the day tended to sensationalize the information and some reported information was inaccurate based upon trial testimony.

The community was divided into two camps and both held their beliefs strongly.

The nature of the conflicting testimony indicates that at least some parties lied under oath, either in an attempt to hide their own involvement or to guarantee the conviction of a party that they honestly believed was guilty.

"Because of" or "in spite of" the final trial verdict, the legal system in Mississippi at that time worked in the manner in which it was intended. The judges, prosecution and defense lawyers performed admirably in almost all situations. This was not a "The Night the Lights Went Out in Georgia" scenario that Hollywood loves to perpetuate about the rural South.

Pending the discovery of some long lost written confession, (a death bed confession has been rumored) we will never know who killed Janie Sharp. Without documentable proof, besmirching a man's good name and character, a man who would now be long dead and unable to defend against such charges would be irresponsible.

I have tried to present the facts as clearly as possible. Whenever there was conflicting information or testimony, I attempted to indicate this. Some issues have never been raised or examined closely and I will attempt to do so in this narrative. It should also be remembered that there was not one unsolved murder but three; Janie Sharp, Walter Permenter and Ben Walker.

Speculation as to who the guilty party or parties might be in all these cases has been a favorite pastime of many over the years. Names have surfaced, tales of anonymous confessions, rumors of a deathbed confession and repetition of second and third hand reports from grandparents, uncles and cousins long deceased keep the mystery and debate alive and well. This is likely how it should remain. Private surmises as to guilt or innocence should remain just that – private.

I would be amiss if I didn't give credit to two compilations about the Janie Sharp event. THE TRIAL for the MURDER of PERNINAH JANIE SHARP by Lucille Wood and TRIAL OF SWINTON PERMENTER FOR THE MURDER OF MISS JANIE SHARP JULY 21,1910 by Ruby C. Hurt. Both of these books are available for viewing at the Winston County Library in Louisville, Mississippi and I encourage those who are interested to take a closer look at these compilations of news reports and trial transcripts.

1. RURAL HILL

It was the summer of 1910. The Civil War was a distant memory and World War One was not yet on the horizon. Life seemed slow and quiet in rural Mississippi, especially to a teenage girl. But American life – even life in Rural Hill, Mississippi was changing much faster than most could ever imagine. The country was just beginning to embrace the 20th Century with its industry and technology and turmoil.

The new decade seemed to bring new firsts every month in aviation; fastest flight, greatest height, crossing of the English Channel, first passenger flight, first seaplane, first night flight, first takeoff from a sea going vessel and as harbingers of things to come, the first patent for a machine gun placement in an aircraft and the first bombs dropped in flight.

April saw the death of America's first true literary icon, Samuel Langhorne Clemens and the return of Halley's Comet after a 75-year absence. Clemens (Mark Twain) was born shortly after the comet's appearance in 1835 and died only a day after it reached its closest proximity to Earth in 1910. The year before his death, Twain was quoted as *"I came in with Halley's Comet in 1835. It is coming again next year, and I expect to go out with it. It will be the greatest disappointment of my life if I don't go out with Halley's*

Comet. The Almighty has said, no doubt: "Now here are these two unaccountable freaks; they came in together, they must go out together."

Politically and socially, the nation was changing as well. Baseball was king and Cy Young was the crown prince as he recorded his 500th win on July 19th. And just two weeks before that – the social order of the country was challenged when a black man, Jack Johnson defeated the white Heavyweight Champ James J. Jeffries with a knockout in the 15th round.

There was unrest as well as October would bring what many regard as the first case of domestic terrorism in the country as a bomb ripped through the offices of the Los Angeles Times.

All of these things were very distant to the farmers and workmen in the tiny communities spread across Mississippi and the South. These bits and pieces of interest arrived once or twice a week in newspapers from such exotic places as Memphis or Jackson. They may have peaked an occasional interest beneath the glow of a coal oil lamp or on a front porch on a Sunday afternoon but were little more than distractions to folks who lived and struggled to succeed upon the land. Few could envision how a flying contraption or a sporting event could have any significant impact on their lives.

But some things were changing even across the most rural parts of the South. A few folks had telephones in their homes although most had to travel to the community store to make or take a phone call. There were a few "horseless carriages" but the mule was still the most important tool on the farm. In the rolling hills of east Mississippi, farm size was limited by a family's ability to work it so the volume of land under cultivation was generally small even for those with broods of children or the benefits of tenant farmers and sharecroppers.

The Rural Hill Community in western Winston County wasn't much different than the hundreds of others scattered across the state and Winston County. In many ways, Rural Hill was indistinguishable from Mill Creek, Coopwood, Hinze, Marydell, Liberty, Fearn Springs and the forty odd others that dotted the county – strategically located every few miles based upon distance and the flow and flood patterns of any number of creeks and minor rivers.

Situated not far from the historic Natchez Trace that ran through neighboring Attala County, the Rural Hill area continued to be sparsely populated until the late 1800's.

The Trace began as a buffalo trail, first used by the multitude of Native American tribes of the area and then as a route for returning raft men taking that long walk back to Nashville and points beyond after floating their goods downriver to the settlement of Natchez.

Sometimes known as the "Devil's Backbone", tales from the heyday of the Trace - of buried treasure, highwaymen and the infamous Harp brothers were certainly common in the early days of the settlement. In latter days, stories of captured Yankee gold and tales of midnight visits of the James gang and their possible family connections in the area were told in hushed tones.

A post office, two general stores, a spoke factory, a two room school house and the Rural Hill Methodist Church were central to the small farms raising cotton for sale, corn and hay for livestock and vegetables for personal consumption. Land in the area was first purchased in 1838 and more settlers came to the area in 1860. These included the Blaine, Lowery, Williams and Ray families.

The makeup of Rural Hill served the community well on a daily basis until the need or desire overtook folk and a visit to the metropolises of Louisville or Kosciusko was required.

Louisville was the county seat of Winston County and boasted a growing population of 1181 in 1910. Situated fourteen miles east of Rural Hill, Louisville had its beginnings as early as 1828 when the entire area was still Indian territory. After the Treaty of Dancing Rabbit in 1830 and the resettlement of most of the Choctaw Indians from the area, Louisville was incorporated in 1836.

The area was relatively unscathed by the Civil War except for the loss of many young men who had quickly volunteered for the Confederacy. The only significant local contact with the dreaded "Yankees" occurred in 1863 as Grierson's Raiders passed through the area in route to Baton Rouge. The raid would later become the subject of a Hollywood movie titled "The Horse Soldiers" starring John Wayne and William Holden.

By 1910, Louisville had recently experienced significant growth with the arrival of the railroad just five years prior. The vast forests of giant pines and hardwoods in the southern half of the state had encouraged rail construction in the late 1800's but the railroad had managed to bypass much of the central part of Mississippi until after the turn of the century. Designated at mile marker 219.3, by 1909, Louisville was served by the New Orleans Mobile & Chicago Railroad.

Rail brought easier access to cotton markets but that benefit was limited. Winston County was not the land of rich dark soil like the Mississippi Delta to the west or the Black Prairie just to its east. Its rolling hills and swamps were not conducive to the planting of vast fields of cotton. These facts combined with the recent and ongoing invasion of the boll weevil limited cotton production. Folks in Winston County and Rural Hill were never able to reap the riches of white gold while sitting on the veranda of their plantation home.

For some, timber was a fine alternative. The deforestation of south

Mississippi and the country's continued demand for lumber served to create a strong and steady market for the shortleaf pines that grew so well in the red clay soils of east central Mississippi.

Saw mills and the logging industry provided much needed cash for the area and created fortunes in the 20th century for a few. Over the years, better management practices, suitable topography and red soil that can produce pine trees like no other place in the country have perpetuated that industry into modern times.

But in 1910, farmers could survive and even prosper with hard work in this land. One farm family that seemed to do well in the Rural Hill community was the Sharp family. The William (Will) Clifton Sharp farm was located approximately one and a half miles southwest of Rural Hill Church. The comfortable house was situated on what is now known as the Neal Ray Road and was home to William Clifton Sharp, his wife, Martha Ezell Ball Sharp, and eight surviving children in 1910. At least one child, a daughter, died in infancy.

One of those children was a popular young woman named Perninah Jane. Known to most as "Janie", she was eighteen in the summer of 1910. Like many rural cultured young women, she was well-mannered and religious. She was an expert seamstress and had some musical training. According to various accounts, she was a strong, healthy girl who caught the eyes of several young men. The only known photos of Janie show a dark haired young woman with strong features.

Later newspaper reports and court testimony indicated that she was engaged to a young man named Earl Ray from another prominent farm family in the Rural Hill area. Over the years, that report has been disputed by some. Regardless, it is believed that she was well liked, well thought of by her peers and elders and had every expectation of a traditional but happy future. Those expectations ended suddenly and tragically on a hot July afternoon on a lonely rural road just outside of Rural Hill, Mississippi.

2. THE MURDER

It was a warm Thursday afternoon (July 21) and Janie had just helped her mother, Martha, clean away the dishes from the noon meal and straighten the house. The men folk in the family had returned to the fields. July was long past planting time but the fieldwork never ended as cotton needed chopping and middles needed to be "laid by" with the plow and mule.

As was likely a regular habit, Janie took the opportunity to travel to the little post office and general stores in Rural Hill where she could pick up the family's mail, make a few purchases, likely socialize with whomever she met along the way and be home in time to help her mother prepare the evening meal.

Rural Free Delivery (RFD) was officially established in 1896 but it was 1901 before rural delivery came to Mississippi and it was a slow process. Full rural delivery had not yet reached Rural Hill in the summer of 1910. That regular trip to the P.O. served a social purpose and was as much a part of life as Sunday church attendance.

Taking her parasol and a delicate handkerchief that would be key to the story, Janie walked the one and a half miles to Rural Hill. Her mother indicated that Janie had planned to purchase a few dress goods. There was some indication that instead of returning immediately home, she intended to stop at the home of Cyrus Ray to do some dressmaking. (In various reports, Cyrus Ray was indicated as not only an uncle to Janie but also as an uncle to her fiancée, Earl Ray.)

Her route took her along Commodore Road. Little more than a narrow dirt wagon path, Commodore Road was bordered at times by a small creek branch that by July was only a dry bed with occasional small pools of water. The path was predominantly shaded as it wound through hardwood thickets and skirted small fields.

Nothing out of the ordinary occurred as Janie conducted her business and made her purchases. When she left the Williams' General Store around three o'clock she was observed by several individuals who noted that she had her parasol, two small packages, a copy of The Weekly Commercial Appeal, two letters for the family and a handkerchief used to wrap a few coins in her possession.

 According to later trial testimony, Janie told at least one individual that she intended to stop by a neighbor's home and make a phone call. The assumption was that this would likely be the Cyrus Ray home where she had told her mother she might stop.

She never made it to the Ray's property nor was there any indication as to why or who she may have intended to call. When Janie left that tiny village of Rural Hill in mid-afternoon on July 21, 1910, she was never seen alive again by anyone other than the person or persons who took her life.

When Janie had not returned by late afternoon, her mother became concerned, left her chores and walked to Rural Hill in search of her. Not finding Janie along the way and discovering at the general store that she had indeed headed toward home, her concern grew.

By the time darkness fell that evening, men from all over the community had formed search parties and were scouring the countryside looking for Janie.

Over the years, different reports, gossip and conflicting trial testimony began to confuse the tale at this point. The preponderance of the evidence supports the following events:

It was near dusk when the search for Janie began as groups of men gathered predominantly on Commodore Road. Telephone lines across the communities of Rural Hill and nearby Hinze were humming with the news of her disappearance and requests for men to join the search. A long and unproductive night lay before them.

In the early hours of the search, some believed that Janie had disappeared of her own accord. While never directly stated in later trial testimony, it was obvious by their actions that some in the community believed that Janie may have eloped with someone other than her current fiancée, Earl Ray. Some reports indicated that Will Sharp (Janie's father) contacted the Winston County Circuit Clerk that evening to find out if a marriage license had been issued. This seems strange given that Earl Ray, her proclaimed fiancée was an early member of the search party. Either this call was made prior to Mr. Sharp's knowledge of Earl Ray's presence or he had reason to believe that Janie had interest in another young man.

One of the men aiding in the search for Janie was Doctor William M. Clemmons, a longtime resident of the community. Records indicate that he was a dentist not a medical doctor and that he had served at one time as the postmaster at Rural Hill. Prior to joining the search, Dr. Clemmons made an attempt to contact the local Methodist minister named Oaks, thinking that perhaps Janie had eloped as well. He was not able to locate the minister and no indication was ever provided as to why he thought that elopement was a possibility. It is possible that Clemmons was acting upon the request of Janie's father.

As night fell, the difficulty of the unorganized effort was compounded by darkness. Many groups of men searched without the benefit of lights or torches. While a large area of fields and woods were scoured, there was little pattern to the search. As the moonlight waned and sporadic rain began to fall, the party grew weary and frustrated. Sometime between 2:00 and 3:00 am, plans were made to defer the search until daylight on Friday morning.

Lee Sharp, Janie's older brother, returned to the search alone, well before the others at around 6:00 am that morning. He returned to Commodore Road, only about a quarter mile from the Sharp home and concentrated on an overgrown area on the west side of the path. He followed a shallow ravine leading to a small branch of water. It was here that he found the body of his sister, Janie.

Information conflicts a bit here. Some indicated that upon finding the body, Lee Sharp fainted and it was several minutes before he came to and began shouting for help. In court testimony, Lee denied this but did admit to losing his composure before crying out to others who had since resumed the search.

Janie's body was partially submerged in the branch in a muddy pool of water. Her throat had been slashed from ear to ear and there was evidence that she had been struck in the head with considerable force. Some reports using graphic descriptions, stated that her head indicated tremendous damage, while later testimony at trial seemed to indicate that she had been struck possibly with the butt of a pistol. There was little blood in and around the pool of water which suggested that she was killed by the blow to the head before her throat was slashed or that she had been killed elsewhere and the body placed here after her death.

Rape was a term not used in any of the news reports. Given the sensibilities of the time, its use would not have been considered appropriate. It was expected that the reader could draw their conclusions from the use of terms such as "assault" and "her person had been violated." While sexual assault was a forgone conclusion, it was never addressed specifically in the investigation and trials.

Near the body were found her packages from the store and the Commercial Appeal newspaper and letters. Her parasol lay between her knees. Witnesses testified that the handkerchief that she was known to carry was not among these items.

The scene was undoubtedly gruesome and Janie's father and brother were distraught. One member of the party offered his raincoat to cover the body. It is likely that her father could no longer bear the sight of his daughter's body lying in that dank, muddy pool. He gathered her remains and returned to the family home. Upon learning of her daughter's death, Mrs. Sharp became despondent and family and neighbors feared for her health.

Calls were made and the Winston County Sheriff A.P. Hull and a number of men from the town of Louisville were headed to the scene by midmorning. Lacking bloodhounds, the sheriff in neighboring Attala County was contacted and by noon, a handler from Kosciusko and his dog were on the scene.

Throughout the morning, a crowd had gathered at the Sharp farm; many shading themselves underneath the long front gallery of the home while speculating and casting suspicious glances among themselves. Only a few doubted that the murderer was a member of the community and most likely someone present. Questions were forming and speculations about behavior during the search, along with past conversations about Janie and her family and old grudges and loyalties were leading some to form quick opinions about one young man in the crowd.

But for now, a family was left to mourn the loss of a young, vibrant daughter. Perninah Jane Sharp was to be buried the next day - Saturday, July 23, 1910 in a rural cemetery a few miles away. She was to lay next to her little sister who had passed away fifteen years earlier.

OBITUARY

MISS JANIE SHARP

The Memory of Miss Janie Sharp.

The 21st and 22 days of July 1910, was the saddest and most sorrowful days that ever came to our neighborhood and the surrounding communities in the past history.

On the afternoon of July, the 21st while Miss Janie Sharp was returning from the Post Office all alone, not thinking of the great and sad fate that was to be her doom, but gladly fulfilling her task of duty kind hearted and true, but alas by the hand of some foul assassin the sweet spirit of Miss Janie was forced to take its flight from loved ones and friends and world of sin and sorrow, back to God who gave this life. It was oh so sad, almost enough to freeze the blood in our veins to see where she was so brutally murdered, all alone, no loved ones or friends to come to her aid or rescue.

Little did she think that lovely afternoon while the Great light of the world was shedding his golden rays of light and bathing our lovely south land with his warm smiles, making the sweet flowers and forest look lovely and gay, that she would be taken home the next morning, a cold murdered corps, oh, how sad to know such was the case and such was her sad fate, but she passed from this earth to join the redeemed throng and sing redemptions holy song. Her sweet voice will be heard no more by those she loved and helped. She will be seen no more in the home and her place in the church is vacant, but we know where to find her, for she has gone to that happy home above, we miss her, oh, we miss her for her place in the Sunday school is vacant and oh how we miss her there for her sweet smiles and kind words always cheered us on.

She was born April 14th 1892 in Winston County near Center Ridge Church, she had lived in the Rural Hill neighborhood where she was murdered two and a half years. How this dear one is missed no one can ever know. But it should draw us all nearer to heaven to lose our loved one. If we have faith in the precious one who said, Let not your heart be troubled; ye believe in God, believe also in me. She joined the Methodist church at Rural Hill in 1908 and was a consistent and faithful member. The Funeral service was conducted by Brother T.L. Oaks at Center Ridge Church, where the sad and grief stricken family together with a large concourse of relatives and sympathying friends saw the mortal remains put to rest, there to await the happy resurrection of the kind and true. She has left her pilgrimage on earth, where she suffered the sad and awful death and gone to the house in the skies prepared for those who loved the Lord. It is a comfort to know that she has gone to a home, where there is no suffering, no pain, no sorrow, no grief but all joy. There is rest, there is peace, there she can pluck sweet flowers from the beautiful garden of heaven and rest by the pure river of the water of life, clear as crystal proceeding out of the throne of God.

She was a kind and true member of the Farmer's Educational and Cooperative Union of America and be it resolved that we extend our deepest heartfelt sympathy to the grief stricken father, mother, brothers and sister.

May the blessings of God wait upon them and the Sun of Glory shine around their hearts, may the gates of plenty, honor, and happiness be always open to them, may strife disturb not their days nor sorrow distress their nights; and finally may the Savior's blood wash them from all impurities and prepare them to enter into the land of everlasting felicity.

3. THE SUSPECT

The crime was brutal and perpetrated upon a young woman that all in the community knew well. Many were related to Janie, some attended school, church, socials and picnics with her as well. Many were there when her body was discovered and saw the torment of a father as he came upon that horrific scene just a few hours before. The men gathered at the Sharp home were in an ugly mood.

There was no indication of any strangers in the community that could have committed this crime and there was no evidence to place blame upon any of the blacks in the area. The killer had to be one of them.

Suspicions almost immediately turned to a young man named Swinton Permenter. Swinton was a teenager of similar age (not yet eighteen) as Janie and the youngest of as many as eight children of Edward Permenter, another local farmer. There are few descriptions of Swinton other than that he was tall, dark-haired and handsome. The only known photograph published was a small inset image in the Commercial Appeal that showed a clean shaven, dapper young man dressed in suit and tie with a fedora perched rakishly atop a mop of curly hair.

It is possible that Swinton was just not well liked by some in the community. There was talk that he lusted after Janie, that he had even made some crude comments in the past about his desire for her. Some claimed that he held bad feelings toward the family, Janie's father, in particular, because he refused to allow Swinton to pursue Janie's affections.

And then there was another rumor - a rumor that was repeated in at least one newspaper in the days after the murder that undoubtedly cast immediate suspicion upon the young man. Swinton's reputation was shaded by a lingering accusation of an attempted assault upon a young girl. Reports were that he had been suspected and even tried for an attack (probably of a sexual nature) upon a seven or ten-year-old child. The rumor was never fully substantiated and the time and place was never indicated although the name of the young victim was disclosed.

Swinton's reputed behavior before, during and after the search aroused suspicion amongst the crowd as well. It became known that he had been at a swimming hole on Lobutcha Creek that flowed between Rural Hill and the community of Hinze with several other young men that afternoon. At some point they separated. This could have placed him near the scene of the crime in the general time frame of the murder.

When the alarm was raised that Janie was missing, almost all of the able men of the community rushed to aid in the search. A pair of men went to the Permenter home and the nearby home of Swinton's uncle in the early hours of the search to ask if anyone had seen Janie and to ask Swinton to assist. They claimed to have not found Swinton even though in later trial testimony, his sister claimed that he had returned home from the field where he had been plowing and had arrived sometime between 5:00 and 6:00 pm.

A local man, Tom McCool joined the search as darkness approached. One of the first things he did was go to the Permenter house in search of Swinton. He was not there. A short time later he encountered Swinton and his uncle O.L. Permenter * about a half mile from the Permenter home walking on Commodore Road.

McCool asked "Why ain't you assisting in the search for Janie?" Swinton seemed hesitant, stating "Well, wait until I go home and get a horse to ride and I'll go with you." McCool pointed out that he was walking and that Swinton didn't need a horse either.

After some persuasion, Swinton agreed to join him. It would be sometime around 10:00 pm before Swinton joined a group of men including Lee Sharp along the Commodore Road.

Lee felt that Permenter behaved strangely during the search. When several men in the party suggested searching a particular patch of undergrowth on the west side of the road, Swinton was reputed to say "Boys, it's no use going in there, I've hunted those woods thoroughly." This particular patch later proved to be the location of Janie's body.

The area wasn't searched at that time and the men continued their hunt for Janie in other areas. Later that night, again according to testimony, Permenter made suggestions to search areas in the opposite direction of where the body was eventually found – "Something in my heart tells me she's back that way."

When the searchers returned the next morning after Janie's body had been found. Swinton Permenter was in the group but others still felt his behavior was unusual. He lay down near a sapling tree away from all the other men and showed little interest until someone remarked that the law would most certainly be bringing bloodhounds to attempt to track the killer. This statement aroused Permenter who seemed eager to let everyone know that he had been searching in those woods and that any bloodhound was likely to track his scent as well as the killer's. He repeated a similar statement later in the morning at the Sharp home.

After following the crowd of men to the Sharp home and as they awaited the arrival of Sheriff Hull, Swinton left with another man, Terrell Suggs, and returned to his home.

While waiting for a coat he had asked to borrow, Suggs observed Swinton come to the porch with a pan of water, wash himself and enter a side room of the home where he changed clothes and shoes. Swinton later returned to the Sharp farm with other family members in a wagon.

The crowd around the Sharp home had been building throughout the morning as the news of Janie's death spread. Talk continued not only about Swinton Permenter but two other young men fell under suspicion as well. Alonzo Burchfield and Walter Cummings had been at that swimming hole with Permenter on the previous afternoon. Their association with Swinton and the fact that they were each other's alibi didn't sit well with some.

There is no direct eyewitness information about the mood and attitude of the crowd during those hours but it is likely that the community had already begun to separate themselves into two camps – those who had faith in Swinton and those who cast a suspicious eye his way.

The sheriff and his men visited the crime scene and took what evidence they could find. A local Justice of the Peace named R.B. McAlilly was present prior to the removal of the body and he asked Dr. Clemmons to examine Janie's corpse. Clemmons later provided a description of the position of the body and the nature of her wounds to the Sheriff at the scene.

Janie had been struck in the head with a blunt object, possibly the butt of a pistol. It was a horrific blow and likely caused her death. The killer then cut her throat from ear to ear and it appeared that she had been stabbed several time under the chin in an attempt to assure her death.

A number of shoe prints were also discovered. Some were obviously those of Janie but others were surmised to be those of the killer. A deputy cut a witch hazel stick and used it to measure the length of the male's print.

There was never any information or testimony concerning the crime scene directly or if the actions of the searchers might have contaminated any evidence. No evidence was ever submitted to confirm that the prints were actually those of the killer and not of someone else who had been at the scene.

By noon, the bloodhounds had arrived. The sheriff from Attala County and J.T. Hanna from Kosciusko soon arrived with a hound named Ruth Hindoo. Hanna claimed to be a third generation dog trainer and he had faith in the dog's ability even though the animal was only fourteen months old.

Hanna started the dog where Janie's body was found. The dog tracked north up the branch about forty yards and along the east side of the branch. Here Hanna and the sheriffs' noted an area where the ground was scuffed. The dog moved away from the branch in a southeasterly direction and the party observed several sets of footprints at different locations. The prints on at least two separate occasions were determined to be both a man's and a woman's.

Ruth Hindoo continued tracking south and approached the farm of Ed Permenter. As the dog reached the yard, Hanna checked her at the gate but soon released her again. She moved away from the house and out into the road where she scented a group of men and then returned to the house and barn lot. She trailed the scent around the lot, the stable and the barn and returned to the front gate and reared upon it.

At this point, Ed Permenter, Swinton's father met them at the gate and Walter Permenter, Swinton's older brother appeared on the porch of the house with a gun in his hand. Hanna later testified that he believed that Walter wanted to shoot him or the dog.

The dog returned to a group of five men standing nearby. In the center was Swinton Permenter. The dog looked at him, threw his head around to his trainer and scented Swinton.

This was enough for Sheriff Hull. Knowing that Swinton had returned home and changed clothes, a search was made to find them. Upon entering the side room, they found the clothes he had worn previously and in a pocket- a Barlow knife, a piece of tobacco and two handkerchiefs- a man's and a woman's. Based upon the dog's behavior and the suspicion of the origin of the woman's handkerchief, Swinton Permenter was taken into custody.

O.L. was sometimes referred to as Ol' Permenter.

4. NO TRIAL NEEDED

By the time the bloodhound Ruth Hindoo had trailed the scent to the Permenter home and directly scented Swinton Permenter, the crowd gathered was slowly but surely turning into a mob. Many were convinced of Permenter's guilt and there were rumblings that a trial wasn't necessary. Emotions were high due to the horrible nature of the crime and its proximity. The victim was a young woman and one of their own.

Sheriff Hull and his men began to believe that a lynching was a real possibility and feared that they could not control the crowd of men. By whatever means available, probably from the Permenter home, Hull telephoned back to Louisville and requested more men.

Hull took Swinton into custody along with Alonzo Burchfield and Walter Cummings who had been with Permenter at the swimming hole the afternoon before.

They began the long fourteen-mile journey back to Louisville with an angry mob of roughly seventy-five men trailing behind. The additional men requested by the sheriff met them along the way.

Tensions did not ease upon their arrival in Louisville. The men were in custody but a crowd continued to gather and rumble outside the Winston County Courthouse throughout the afternoon. Later newspaper reports (Winston County Journal) indicated that talk of lynching the suspects was circulating throughout the day.

Responsible parties (likely including the circuit court judge who happened to be in town for a session) made the decision to get the suspects out of town for their safety. At 11:00 pm on Friday, July 22, Permenter, Burchfield and Cummings were taken to the depot in Louisville and placed on a train procured for the sole purpose of transport to Winona, Ms.

Roughly forty-five miles away, Winona was chosen for several reasons. It was far enough away to ease the tensions, it was an easy access by train and most importantly, it was the home of Judge McLean, the 5th Circuit Judge, who was likely to be the judge to preside over the case and any grand jury indictment.

Permenter's clothing and the items found in his pockets were held as evidence. Newspaper reports were the only record of the handling of the evidence and the accuracy of information was suspect. The Winston County Journal indicated that the clothes appeared to have been washed but that there was evidence of blood on some of the clothing. The Journal also reported that the County Attorney, J. B. Gully had taken the items to Mississippi A&M College (now Mississippi State University) to be analyzed with a chemical test to determine if any blood was human in nature.

Over the next few days and weeks, newspaper reports began to sensationalize the event. In modern day terms, the story went viral and appeared in papers as far away as the West Coast, New York and all over the South.

Many reports were inaccurate and based on hearsay information. Timelines were inaccurate, names and ages of the parties involved were also inaccurately reported. Speculation as to the nature of Swinton's and Janie's relationship were reported as fact and the lynching threat was almost certainly exaggerated.

By Saturday morning, July 23, Permenter, Burchfield and Cummings were safely tucked away in jail in Montgomery County. Permenter was considered the main suspect and it is likely that Burchfield and Cummings were being held to guarantee their safety and to possibly elicit testimony.

The Sharp family was in mourning. The condition of the body and the summer heat led the family to arrange Janie's funeral on Saturday as well. Janie's younger sister, Nellie Lenora had been interred at the cemetery at Center Ridge Methodist Church located just a few miles to the east of Rural Hill and Janie was placed beside her.

Lee Sharp, Janie's older brother was convinced of Swinton Permenter's guilt. That afternoon after his sister's funeral, he returned to the scene of the crime looking for further evidence. While not attributed to Lee Sharp, the Winston County Journal reported on July 29, 1910, information that likely was relayed by him and possibly confirmed later by the Sheriff:

Tracks were found leading from the road to Cyrus Ray's home that lead into the nearby woods and down a branch. It was speculated that the initial assault occurred here as Janie turned off Commodore Road and headed for her uncle's home. It appeared that Janie escaped her attacker and ran for a few yards before she was caught again. She escaped a second time and ran farther before being overtaken again where evidence of a major struggle could be seen. It was believed that she escaped for a third time as she ran back toward the road before her attacker caught her one last time and struck her with the blow that took her life.

It was never clear if this location was the spot where her body was found or if the killer moved the body into the branch and the pool of water in an attempt to hide it or destroy evidence.

Regardless of who was responsible, Janie had put up a strong struggle for her life. At least for now, a suspect was in custody and it appeared that most were convinced that seventeen-year-old Swinton Permenter was guilty of the crime.

5. FIRST TRIAL

Little is known about the next few days. No documentation related to the sheriff's investigation exists but it is likely that time was spent in and around the Rural Hill community gathering evidence and interviewing anyone who might have any information about the crime or Swinton Permenter, Walter Cummings or Alonzo Burchfield.

In another unresolved twist to the case, The Kosciusko Star Ledger reported that on July 25th, the Monday after the murder, a fourth man had been arrested in the case. This report was confusing and not substantiated by any other papers. No details were provided and the man's name was listed as Charley Horn in the body of the report but listed as Charlie Lake in the headline. This arrest was not mentioned in later trial testimony and it is likely that this individual may have simply been sought and questioned as a witness in the case.

Any investigation was likely complicated by the bloodthirsty mood that pervaded the community. Much energy and effort was expended in calming those who were calling for immediate justice. There were some reports that Judge McLean spoke to the mob of men gathered at the time of the arrests and assured them that a speedy trial would take place. It is apparent that some felt that a jury should be immediately empaneled. When McLean later adjourned the court session already in place and returned to his home in Winona, some felt betrayed and let it be known that if a trial didn't take place soon, they would take matters into their own hands. Over time, cooler heads prevailed in the community. There is some evidence that Will Sharp did much to calm the situation.

Rumors multiplied and tensions between families and neighbors were high. Some came to the defense of the young man, Swinton Permenter. Others would have likely killed him on sight.

Three young men were in custody but the evidence seemed to show that only one man committed the crime and most believed that man was Permenter. A significant amount of circumstantial evidence existed:

A handkerchief believed to be the victim's was found in Permenter's possession. The Sharp family confirmed that the handkerchief found in Swinton's pocket belonged to Janie. She was known to have it in her possession before the murder and it was missing from the crime scene.

The tracks found at the murder scene were a close match to Permenter's shoe size. A sheriff's deputy had cut a stick to measure the track and it would be submitted as evidence.

His general proximity to the area and time of the crime did not exclude him. This was likely the reason that Cummings and Burchfield were taken into custody as well.

The bloodhound tracked from the crime scene to the Permenter home and seemed to specifically scent upon Swinton.

His strange and, at least to some, misleading behavior during the search for Janie was suspicious.

There were rumors also. Some claimed that Swinton Permenter made some remarks indicating his desire for Janie's affection and that he had made some vague threats against Janie's father, possibly because he didn't approve of Permenter.

This circumstantial evidence against this young man was significant - if it was accurate. But there were also gaps and questions in the evidence or at least in the investigation:

Permenter's clothes had been submitted to a nearby college for examination of blood evidence. An official report had not been completed. While a witness observed him washing on the morning after the murder, there was no clear evidence presented to show that his clothing had been washed.

Based upon Lee Sharp's observations, Janie put up a significant struggle for her life. This could have resulted in marks, bruises or scratches upon the killer. None were ever referenced on Permenter.

Some reported that Permenter was carrying a pistol on the night of the search. This would seem significant given that it was speculated that the blow to Janie's head may have been from the butt of a pistol. The weapon was never mentioned again in trial testimony.

There was also no mention of a knife. Janie's throat had been cut from ear to ear and apparently stabbed as well. Other than the Barlow knife in Swinton's pocket, a knife was never recovered or submitted into evidence.

****

Newspaper reports were muddled. The Winston County Journal, the Kosciusko Star Ledger, Kosciusko Herald and the Jackson Daily printed detailed reports on the crime but tended to sensationalize the events and at least one clearly stated a belief in not only Permenter's guilt but that of Burchfield and Cummings as well. One reported that Circuit Judge George A. McLean had recessed court and attended the scene of the crime with the sheriff. This was never verified but seems to be a likely scenario due to the fact that McLean was in Louisville presiding over a grand jury at the time of the murder.

On Wednesday following the murder, Sheriff Hull caught the train to Winona to interview the suspects and confer with Judge McLean. He returned later that day with Walter Cummings and Alonzo Burchfield. There was no evidence connecting them to the crime and the sheriff believed that it was safe to allow them to return to their homes. Walter Cummings was released unconditionally while Burchfield was released under bond requiring him to appear before an upcoming grand jury. The opinion was that he would be a significant material witness in the case. Swinton Permenter remained in a Montgomery County jail until his trial.

Permenter had his supporters. Funds were raised to pay for his defense, attorneys were hired and they prepared for the biggest trial ever held in Winston County. Permenter was not released on a bond and there was little for him to do but consult with his lawyers as the days dragged on during a long hot Mississippi summer.

Even in 1910, the legal process was deliberate. It would be nearly two months before another grand jury could be convened. Without effort, it could have taken much longer. In this, Swinton was fortunate. Judge McLean made good on his promise to speed the process when he called for a special grand jury on September 8th and set the date for September 19th for the main purpose of an indictment of Swinton Permenter.

Several cases were heard at this time but on the morning of

September 19, 1910, Swinton Permenter appeared before Judge McLean in a Winston County courtroom.

No detailed court records exist of this event. Court minutes only provide the results of any decision. Twenty citizens had been selected to serve as grand jurors earlier in the month. The names of many of these jurors are still common names across the county. A.H. Halfacre was the foreman and others included: Barnhill, Cooper, Pearson, Kelly, Holmes, Moore, Spence, Dawson, Pope (2), Clay, Kinard, Dempsey, Tisdale, Taggart, Roberson, Boyd, Price and Miller.

The Circuit Court minutes read: *The State of Mississippi vs Swinton Permenter: charge of murder. This day came the District Attorney who prosecutes for the State and the defendant Swinton Permenter in his own proper person and being represented by counsel and being arraigned on a bill of indictment charging him with murder, pleads not guilty therefore the Court remanded him to jail.*

Contrary to modern day criminal trials, things advanced quickly. There would be no change of venue. The trial was set in Louisville in early October, 1910. The case was to be heard before Judge George A. McLean with prosecutors, Lamb, Gully and Jones and local defense attorneys, Rodgers, Brantley, and Hopkins.

The trial began on October 3 as the defense asked for a change of venue. This request was promptly denied by Judge McLean and jury selection began that morning. A pool of 126 potential jurors was determinedly accepted or rejected until a final jury of twelve was seated. Again the names of jurors still reflect the families of current residents of the community. Some names in the court record are almost indiscernible. The jury consisted of:

Jim Ming, J.W. Edwards, Ike Yarbrough, Calvin Palmer, J. O.

Landrum, M. H. Hanna, Printis (Prentiss) Adcock, A.L. Jackson, H.O. Houston, Frank Hindman, J.A. Hatcher, D.C. Coleman

Because of the spectacular nature of the crime and the bad blood that had developed, Judge McLean empaneled four special bailiffs for the trial and jury: W. H Lavon, C. A. Jones, W.E. Murphy and J. W. Triplett.

It is unfortunate that no transcript of the trial has survived - at least not one that can be found. The only written information available are the court minutes, limited newspaper articles and some references in a later Mississippi Supreme Court ruling. Circuit court records are maintained locally and are not archived at the state level. At least one courthouse demolition and new construction and countless circuit clerks have committed those records to the dust of history.

While there are no records of testimony, there is an extensive witness list that includes as many as sixty-eight called to testify. These include many familiar names: Sharp, Ray, Burchfield, McCool, Shumaker, Steed, Horn and McLeod to name a few. It is interesting to note that none of Swinton Permenter's immediate family is included in this list.

One name not on the witness list was a man named Ben (referred to as Hugh or Dan in some newspaper reports) Walker. Walker was reputed to be from the Mississippi Delta, possibly from the Cleveland area and presented himself as a private detective. He had been known to be in the area shortly after the murder and it is a reasonable assumption that he was hired by the Permenter family to investigate the case and find the guilty party. On at least one occasion, Walker insinuated that he had actually been hired by the Governor of Mississippi, Edmond Noel, to work the case due to its volatile nature.

There is no physical description of Walker, no reference to his age or qualifications as a detective, no background or family connections. Unknown to the community, he did not make a good impression or win friends. While not included on the witness list, there is at least one indication that he did testify in the trial but had little of consequence to say and made a poor impression upon the jury.

The trial began on a Monday and the verdict was reached on the Tuesday of the following week. Court was held on Saturday. Jury selection encompassed much of the first day, October 3 and summations filled the last day, October 11.

On the final day of the trial, reports indicated that the courtroom was packed and included a number of women. Men blocked the aisles and sat in the window wells of the room. Swinton's mother had not attended the trial until the last day when she sat beside her son.

At 9:00 am, the prosecution began its closing arguments. An ex-District Attorney Jones spoke for an hour and urged the jury to perform their duty for Winston County and the State of Mississippi, stating that the physical evidence told the truth in the case and vilifying Permenter in the process.

The defense's statement was conducted by the local Attorney Hopkins who argued that the prosecution had not proved its case or presented a reasonable motive for the crime.

By the afternoon at 1:45 pm on Tuesday, October 11, the case was handed to the jury.

The decision was quickly reached. Over the years, some reported that the jury returned with their verdict in as little as four minutes. This is not accurate. While jurors indicated that the decision was reached on the first ballot, it was 6:00 pm before the jury returned to the courtroom.

Well aware of the ugly mood that pervaded the community, Judge McLean cleared the courtroom before the verdict was read. The jury's decision was passed to the court clerk who read:

We, the jury, find the defendant guilty as charged of the indictment."

In less than three months, Swinton Permenter had been arrested, tried and found guilty of the crime of murder upon Perninah Janie Sharp of Rural Hill Mississippi. There was little doubt that the rush to judgment, the mood of the community and the fear of possible retribution had significant influence on the jury.

The Winston County Journal made much of Swinton Permenter's calm and composure throughout the trial and speculated that this worked against him in the minds of the jury.

"Permenter shows composure and nerve unknown to history, if he is normal and sane as his friends claim he is. During the ten* long days of his trial he sat with perfect composure and stolid indifference, even to the sentence of death. He seemed the least concerned of any in the room, this indifference appearance was so noticeable that it really made the case against him."

Swinton was returned to his cell in the Winston County jail overnight for sentencing the next day. A guard reported to the newspaper that Permenter broke down after the verdict but soon fell asleep.

On the morning of October 12, a request by Permenter's attorneys for a new trial was denied by Judge McLean. Before passing sentence, Judge McLean asked Permenter if he had anything to say.

An emphatic "I AM NOT GUILTY" was his only response.

Based upon the nature and severity of the crime, the sentence was a forgone conclusion. Swinton Permenter was sentenced to hang on November 25, 1910. Gallows were to be constructed by order of the county supervisors for that purpose.

* This is incorrect as the trial actually lasted nine days.

6. THE APPEAL

An appeal of Swinton Permenter's conviction was immediately started for the Mississippi State Supreme Court. With an appeal before the court, his November 25 execution was on hold. In the meantime, Permenter was imprisoned outside of Winston County for safekeeping.

By the 1900's, Mississippi was in the process of adding prison facilities in Rankin County and Sunflower County. In 1903, the original state prison known as "The Walls" was torn down to make room for the new State Capitol Building that was constructed on the site in the center of Jackson. In 1900, the Parchman Plantation in Sunflower County was purchased and was operating by 1905 in the Mississippi Delta. The Rankin Prison Farm was also operational by 1910 near Jackson. It is now the site of the Mississippi State Hospital Psychiatric Facility known to most Mississippians as Whitfield.

Because Swinton's case was under consideration for appeal, he never experienced the hospitality of either of these facilities. He was to spend the next few months at the Hinds County Jail.

Swinton had become a celebrity of sort. The case and trial were reported all over the country and the public wanted to know more about the young man convicted of such a brutal murder. At least one newspaper, The Jackson Daily News, sought out information from guards and prisoners concerning Permenter.

According to an article published on November 15, 1910, Swinton was making a very positive impression upon his jailers and fellow prisoners as well. His "quiet gentlemanly conduct" seemed to win over most to the belief that he was innocent of murder and a victim of circumstance. His jailers spoke highly of him and were quoted extensively in the Jackson Daily article:

"His sleep is never troubled and if this boy is guilty of the crime for which he has been condemned, he is the coldest hearted villain I ever saw. There has never been any act or word- sleeping or waking to indicate him guilty of this murder."

"The only thing that seems to bother him is his father and mother. He writes home nearly every day telling them he is getting along as well as can be expected, but these letters never touch upon the crime for which he is convicted of, except to ask what is being done to trace the murderers of Janie Sharp."

"Permenter is a jovial sort of boy but his confinement is telling on him to some extent. He sleeps about twelve hours at night and is gaining weight but he does not look as well as when he came here. I have been to his cell at night and have never found him awake, he sleeps sound and when he awakes in the morning he seems refreshed and fit for hard work."

"He has discussed the murder of Janie Sharp with me some, as he has with everyone who visits him, but has never said anything that could be construed into even an intimation that he committed the crime. He has, on the contrary said he believed two other fellows committed the crime and these two men from what I understand were active in the prosecution.... He seems to think everything will turn out right in the end and I believe it will."

Swinton would spend the winter of 1910-1911 in the Hinds County Jail and it would be spring before the Mississippi Supreme Court ruled on his case.

In the meantime, things were returning to some level of calm in Winston County and around Rural Hill. Ben Walker had been hired at the behest of the Permenter family. The self- proclaimed private investigator seemed to make little or no progress in the case and apparently was not making a good impression around the area. Many believed that he was simply biding his time and bleeding the family and supporters financially until their money ran out. There are no records of his investigation and no witnesses to explain his activities.

The stress of the murder had a major impact on the Sharp family and Mrs. Sharp, Janie's mother was devastated. The family or at least Mrs. Sharp and the younger children left Rural Hill on October 18, 1910 and returned to the community of McCool in neighboring Choctaw County, a few miles distant from their farm and the scene of the crime. Apparently the family had lived in the little town sometime prior to moving to Rural Hill.

Sometime after that move, Mrs. Sharp published an open letter (likely in the Winston County Journal) to the community. It is interesting to note that in the letter, there was a glaring inconsistency that would not be expected from a mother writing about her children. Janie's named was spelled differently than is shown on public records and on her tombstone. It seems likely that while Mrs. Sharp may have dictated the letter, someone outside of the family wrote the document based on this inaccuracy. It is presented here verbatim:

LETTERS WERE A COMFORT

Dear Mrs. Gray and All the Kind Sisters-Here comes a broken-hearted mother. Sisters, I want to thank each and everyone who sent me letters and I am sorry I can't answer all personally. Please remember I appreciate them just as if I had answered them all. They were so sweet and sympathizing, but dear people, it sometimes seems like my trouble is more than I can bear. Oh, I miss my dear, sweet Jannie ever so much. It's awful to think she had to die like she did, but thank God, she was a pure, sweet girl and I know she is now quietly resting with God. The one sweet consolation I have is I can meet my dear child, and I know I have two sweet angels in heaven. One little babe, three months and three days old died fifteen years ago. I thought that was trouble, but sisters, no one knows what trouble is until they have a child to walk off well and hearty and be brought back murdered as my child was. Dear sisters, after my dear child had suffered this awful death she had one of the sweetest smiles on her dear face and looked like she wanted to tell me all about it. Oh, how I wish she could have told me all about it, but God knows best, and all will be explained someday. Oh, our home is so lonely without Jannie. She was so lively and industrious. She did most all of the housework and cut and did all of the sewing. We surely miss her very much. She was always singing and playing the organ every spare moment, and she was the only grown child I had at home. I have three little children at home now, a boy 14, a girl 11 and one 9, but they are all in school and I will be so lonely. My oldest daughter, whose home is in Oklahoma, has been with us; came very soon after Jannie was taken, but will leave for home tomorrow, and we will miss her and her two sweet little boys. She says she intends to write a letter to the Commercial Appeal when she gets home. I have two married sons, living twelve miles away and another daughter married and living eight miles from me. She has a dear little ten-month old girl and she will spend next week with me and help me get my fall sewing done. Well, we have moved back to our old home, which is in the pretty little town of McCool. We moved Oct. 18, but I left some good, dear friends around Rural Hill and they were so good and kind to us in our great trouble and we can never forget their kindness. We have friends here, too and from the good letters I received, I know I have sympathizing friends all over the states.

Mrs. Carrie Carter of Plattsburg, Miss., was so thoughtful and kind in asking you, sisters to write me and your good words have relieved me of many sad hours. Well, I will bid you all adieu for this time with best wishes for all and our dear paper, I am.

Mrs. Will Sharp

*****

On April 24, 1911, The Supreme Court of Mississippi "reversed and remanded" the verdict issued by the jury in Louisville on October 11 of the previous year against Swinton Permenter. The ruling was primarily based upon flaws in the instructions provided to the jury concerning the application of circumstantial evidence and the concept of reasonable doubt.

After providing a brief synopsis of the initial trial, the court ruled that an instruction given to the jurors was "fatally erroneous." Jurors were instructed that the defendant could be convicted if circumstantial evidence generates full conviction in their mind beyond a reasonable doubt. The Supreme Court held that "full conviction" is not the criteria or degree of proof necessary to convict. Citing other cases, the court held that circumstantial evidence must be weighed with caution and that every other theory except for the guilt of a defendant must be excluded by that evidence.

The Supreme Court held that proper instruction as requested by the appellant was refused related to the weighing of circumstantial evidence and that the jury should have been informed that any fact proven to their satisfaction which was inconsistent with the defendant's guilt constituted reasonable doubt.

In the ruling to reverse and remand, the Supreme Court made the following statement:

The appellant, Swinton Permenter, was convicted of murder and sentenced to hang, and appeals to this court. He was convicted on evidence wholly circumstantial, made up of many different facts and circumstances. There is grave doubt, from the record in this case of appellant's guilt.

Recognizing that this case would likely be tried again, the court refused further comment.

Considering this ruling and the time he had already spent in jail, Permenter would be eligible for bail. On Monday, May 22, 1911, Swinton Permenter was granted bail in the sum of a $10,000 bond. By Tuesday, friends and family had raised sufficient funds to make the bond and Swinton was released from the Hinds County Jail on Wednesday. Reports were that he returned home at least temporarily to the Rural Hill area.

His case would go back to Winston County for a retrial, but a change of venue due to all the publicity was quickly granted and the next trial would be held in the City of Winona in Montgomery County, the place where he had been incarcerated prior to the first trial.

This second trial was scheduled for October, 1911. On the first day of trial, the defense team filed for a continuance due to the absence of several key witnesses for the defense. Reports were that at least five defense witnesses were not present, the key witness being Swinton's sister who was reported gravely ill and unable to testify. Over strong objections by the state, the court ruled to continue the case until its next session in April, 1912.

It would actually be August 1912 before the final trial of Swinton Permenter, more than two years after the murder of Janie Sharp.

The events between the October continuance and the final trial only added to the tragedy and mystery surrounding the whole case. Two additional unsolved murders, possible alternative suspects and bribery charges created doubts, distrust and served to widen the breach between those convinced of Permenter's guilt and those who supported him.

7. BEN WALKER

Bad blood ruled the Rural Hill and Hinze communities throughout the remainder of 1911 and well into 1912 prior to the final trial. The Sharps and the Permenters both had large extended families not only in Rural Hill but in the surrounding areas. Friends and neighbors took sides based upon their connections and loyalties.

Lee Sharp, Janie's older brother was adamant that Swinton Permenter was the man who took his sister's life and felt that some – including Swinton's family members knew more than they had revealed about the case and he had no problem making his feelings public.

The Permenter family was just as strong in their convictions and apparently continued to pay Detective Ben Walker to investigate the case. It is likely that the Permenters felt that providing an alternate theory or suspect would weaken any case against Swinton.

There was without question, a financial drain placed upon the family. Friends of the Permenters apparently provided funding not only for Walker's services but also for Swinton's defense team.

Little is known about Ben Walker. There is no known physical description or reference to his age. His qualifications as an investigator, exactly where he came from and how he became involved in the Janie Sharp affair are unclear, but his short role in the case was mysterious, confounding and tragic.

Some records (Commercial Appeal) indicate that Ben Walker testified in the first Permenter trial. If accurate, in his testimony he claimed to be from Cleveland, Ms. and was "instructed" by the Governor to make inquiries into the crime. The newspaper story indicated that Walker's testimony was inconsequential and that he left a poor impression upon the court.

Most accounts indicate that Walker was actually hired by the Permenter family. He possibly misrepresented himself under oath about his official status or he was later hired by the family in a non-official capacity.

Walker must have spent considerable time in the community and it is apparent that he stayed with a relative of the Permenters, J. E. (Elbert) Vowell, while investigating the case. The distrust of outsiders and his activities on behalf of the Permenters did little to endear him to the general population in and around Rural Hill.

In November, 1911, a little over a year after the first trial and a month after the second trial had been delayed, Detective Ben Walker created a stir in the community when he returned from Greenville, Texas with Thomas Jefferson McElroy and his family. Walker "arrested" McElroy for the murder of Janie Sharp. One newspaper reported that Walker had an order of requisition issued by Governor Noel for McElroy.

McElroy was a young family man and was a previous resident of Rural Hill and strangely enough, a brother-in-law to Earl Ray, Janie's fiancée. He and his family had moved to Texas in September, 1910 shortly after Janie's murder. McElroy had been a member of the search party on the day of Janie's murder. No suspicion had ever been cast upon McElroy prior to this time and his arrest by Walker was met with a great deal of skepticism.

It was apparent that McElroy returned to Mississippi of his own free will. In fact, newspaper reports indicated that his wife and two small children accompanied him and Ben Walker on the train ride from Texas. *(There is some conflicting information here as cemetery records indicate that McElroy's only child died as an infant. This is likely incorrect as other records indicate that he had a young son and daughter)* The whole party spent the night at a Jackson, Ms. hotel before catching a train to nearby McCool and arriving at Cyrus Ray's home late in the evening on Monday, November 13.

The facts aren't directly known but some suspected that Walker concocted a story that cast suspicion on McElroy and the young man returned willingly to clear his name. Others believed that Walker did in fact had information from witnesses that implicated McElroy. McElroy seemed to have no ill will toward Walker and even encouraged his father-in-law, Cyrus Ray, to treat Walker right as he had treated him and his family properly on their trip from Texas.

Upon returning to Rural Hill and depositing the McElroy family with the Rays, Ben Walker disappeared for two days. On Tuesday morning while at the Ray home, he complained of chlorea morbeus (gastroenteritis), left the house and was not seen again until Thursday when he appeared in Louisville and arranged for a preliminary hearing for McElroy on the following Monday.

During this time, a second suspect, Hulett or (Hewlett) Ray, was arrested upon an affidavit of Elbert Vowell, the man that was providing housing for Walker.

On the following Monday morning, Thomas McElroy was the first to appear along with his attorneys before Justice McAlilly. As the hearing began, the state asked for a one-day continuance. Four witnesses that were key to the case were not present.

On Tuesday, the parties returned to the courtroom. By McElroy's side was Will Sharp, Janie's Father.

The County Attorney, J. B. Gully presented no witnesses and quickly asked that all charges be dropped and stated that there was no evidence that these two men (McElroy and Ray) were involved in Janie Sharp's murder.

Will Sharp spoke to a reporter with the Kosciusko Herald: *"I believe in his (McElroy) entire innocence. He knows no more about the murder of my poor child than a stranger. Ray is innocent also. It's a crying shame the way they are arresting innocent persons. It's merely a subterfuge to create sympathy for the crime. I am going to stick to them both and see them through for they are as innocent as a new born babe."*

There is no record of any evidence that Walker may have submitted concerning the two men. McElroy & Ray were released and almost immediately, Ben Walker was arrested and charged with attempting to bribe witnesses. Some indicated that he was charged with perjury as well. Walker claimed that his witnesses were intimidated and afraid to testify but never alluded to any specific witnesses or evidence. He was adamant that he had strong evidence against McElroy.

As a result of these charges, his already questionable reputation was further damaged and it certainly increased animosity toward him and his actions. The local newspaper, The Winston County Journal, attempted to interview Walker after the hearing and made no attempt to hide its contempt for Walker's actions in the case and called for him to be dealt with harshly if the charges proved to be true. The story made newsprint as far away as Mobile, Alabama and the Boston Evening Transcript. These articles stated that a mob had gathered with a desire to storm the Winston County jail and lynch Walker for his actions. While there was certainly animosity in the courtroom toward Walker, the threat of lynching was likely exaggerated.

Walker was scheduled for a hearing on the charges a few days later, but no records indicate if these bribery charges were pursued or later dropped and it was never mentioned in further newspaper reports.

Walker remained in the area throughout the winter of 1911-1912 and it was believed that he continued to work on the case, although he may have pursued other activities as well. While in the area, he continued to stay in the home of Elbert Vowell (who had filed the affidavit against Hewlett Ray), located a few miles south of Rural Hill.

On the Spring evening of March 20, 1912, Ben Walker was at home with Elbert Vowell. The hour was not late but darkness had fallen and the two men were sitting together quietly. Walker was reading by the light of a lamp near a window.

The stillness of that rural homestead was suddenly shattered by a shotgun blast and the sound of breaking glass. Vowell reached for his gun as he saw Walker fall to the floor amongst the broken glass and blood. He ran outside in the darkness and fired at what he believed to be two men riding away on horseback. At some distance, the men returned fire before disappearing into the night.

Elbert Vowell returned to his home and found Detective Ben Walker in a heap on the floor. The shooter had been close- Walker was nearly decapitated by a blast of buckshot.

The current Sheriff Carr was in the state capital on business and the murder was investigated by a Deputy Sheriff Clark and the now ex-Sheriff Hull. They quickly arrived at the scene but found no clues of significance and the investigation went nowhere. Vowell claimed that the perpetrators had fired as many as fifteen shots at him as he pursued them from his home.

Of course, speculations were rampant:

Had someone in the Sharp family or close to the Sharp family had enough of Walker's meddling and attempts to find another suspect and decided to put an end to it?

Had the real killer(s) believed that Walker was close to finding the truth or even had information to prove their guilt and chose to silence him?

Or perhaps Walker's death was not related at all to Janie's murder and his other activities had been the cause of his murder.

There are no details of any further investigation into his death. No one else was wounded and no suspects were ever named in the death of Detective Ben Walker. His body was not claimed by any family members and his involvement in the Janie Sharp case is the only record of his existence. A search of records in Cleveland and Bolivar County reveal no one of the age and race who could possibly be identified as the detective. The common nature of his name and the possible confusion as Ben or Hugh or Dan makes further identification nearly impossible. Ben Walker was buried on March 22, 1912 in the small rural Wood (Smallwood) Cemetery located a few miles southwest of Rural Hill.

8. MISTAKEN IDENTITY?

The second trial of Swinton Permenter for the murder of Janie Sharp had been postponed until late summer of 1912. The venue had been moved from Winston County to Winona in Montgomery County.

As defense lawyers and prosecutors prepared their cases, life went on as usual. There were two tragic events in the Spring of 1912 that stole the newspaper headlines from the case and upcoming trial.

The sinking of the Titanic grabbed world headlines in April. News reports in Mississippi came from the wire services but there was a Mississippi connection. After some confusion, it was determined that a Mississippi man, A.N. Lahaud, was one of the victims. Lahaud was a Biloxi resident with Syrian roots. Reports were that he had been visiting his childhood home in Syria, traveled to Europe and had intended to leave to return to Mississippi around the same time that the *Titanic* sailed for the United States. When lists of survivors and victims began appearing after the wreck, an individual named Sekas Lahoud appeared on listings of the victims. Lahaud's parents, also residents of Biloxi, were not sure that this was their son but it was later confirmed by a family member that Lahaud had indeed been aboard. His body was never recovered.

In a tragedy closer to home, a train carrying Confederate veterans from Texas to a reunion in Macon, Georgia derailed on the New Orleans and Northeastern railroad near Hattiesburg, Mississippi in May. There were as many as fifteen victims including four railroad employees, the engineer and fireman, two women and two small children.

In spite of these events, the trial was still foremost on the minds of Winston County residents. Rumors surfaced that Swinton's older brother, Walter, had information gathered by the now murdered Ben Walker that was instrumental in the case.

Edward Walter Permenter was 12 years older than his brother but of similar build and appearance. The oldest surviving son of the Permenter family (an older brother died at the age of two) Walter was a staunch defender of Swinton.

As the trial approached, Swinton spent the days prior at the home of a family member in Eupora, Mississippi located just to the east of Winona. Whether he had spent considerable time here is unknown but is a strong possibility due to the hostile environment around Rural Hill and McCool. Eugene Shewmake was said to be a brother-in-law to members of the family. There was some confusion in newspaper reports that the name was Shumaker or Shumacher but the local newspaper, The Progress Warden noted that Shewmake was the correct name.

The trial was scheduled for August 5 in nearby Winona. On Friday afternoon, August 2, 1912, Walter Permenter joined his brother Swinton at the Shewmake home. The brothers intended to leave Eupora on the next day, Saturday, and arrive at Winona where the trial was to begin on the following Monday.

The following information came from various sources but the Progress Warden issue of August 8, 1912 (Eupora, Ms.) provided the most detail.

Around nine o'clock on that Friday evening, Swinton retired for the night. A short while later around 10:00 pm, his brother Walter and Shewmake prepared to retire as well. Both went out the back door of the home, Shewmake to empty a waste bucket and Walter to draw some water from the well located on the back porch of the home. Shewmake returned back inside and almost immediately heard a gunshot.

 As he was drawing the water, Walter was struck by a shotgun blast. He was hit in the head, neck and chest by the blast and fell off the porch gasping his last breaths. Reports are that he died within a few moments. Shewmake doused all the lights in the home fearing more shots from the assailant.

The sound of the shotgun blast roused the neighborhood and people quickly appeared and rushed to the scene. No one had seen anything except for one young man, Noel Myers, who claimed to see a single individual running across a vacant lot away from the Shewmake house just moments after the shot was fired. The night passed without any further incident and no clues as to the identity or the whereabouts of the murderer.

By telephone, local authorities began a search that night for bloodhounds to track the assassin. A deputy from nearby Monroe County loaded his dogs in an automobile in the early morning hours and headed to Eupora.

By 8:00 am, the bloodhounds were on the scene and they soon picked up a trail that led southward from the home and around a cotton house at the Eupora Gin Company. The trail continued further south toward Winston County and into the Big Black Swamp located just south of the town of Eupora. The dogs eventually lost the trail in the hills south of town.

By Saturday evening, Walter and Swinton's father, Ed Permenter, three members of the related Vowell family and Mr. W. J. Tabor had arrived to claim the body. Tabor was a store owner in Louisville and was Walter's employer. Later reports indicate that Tabor's Store and several others burned down a few months after the trial under mysterious circumstances.

While in Eupora, the Permenter family discussed Swinton's case and the murder of Walter openly with friends and the local newspaper. In previous discussions early in the day, the Shewmake family expressed their belief that Walter's murder was a case of mistaken identity. They believed that Swinton was the real target. But Ed Permenter and the Vowells had a different theory.

They believed that Walter was the target due to his involvement in the case and intimated that Swinton's brother had evidence and possibly certain papers that had been gathered by Ben Walker that were crucial to his case and would point the finger at the real guilty party or parties.

More intrigue was added to the incident when it was suggested by the Permenter family that at least one man had been missing from the Rural Hill area for most of the previous week, suggesting that he may have been involved in Walter's murder. This man was never publicly identified and there was no apparent follow up to the investigation.

Initial plans were to inter Walter Permenter in the Hopewell Cemetery located in Choctaw County where other family members were buried but by the time the party arrived back in Winston County, arrangements were made to inter the body in the city limits of Louisville. No reason was indicated for this decision but it may have been financial, possibly for concern for the safety of the family under the circumstances or the condition of the body.

On the following Sunday in Eupora, a young boy stumbled upon a shotgun hidden in the cotton house; a breach loading shotgun found inside a tow sack with one spent shell and several others loaded with buckshot. It was speculated that the killer had tied his horse under a shed at the cotton house and fearing capture and questioning did not want to be caught with the murder weapon. Newspaper reports claimed that there were identifying marks on the weapon and it was turned over to local law enforcement. There is no record of further investigation into the matter.

The Eupora newspaper did report that after the murder, the Governor of the State of Mississippi offered a $500 reward for the capture of Walter Permenter's assassin and also for the capture of the killer of Ben Walker.

Edward Walter Permenter had not lived to see his 32nd birthday. He left a wife and three small children. He was buried in the Masonic Cemetery within the City of Louisville.

There are no further records of the investigation in Eupora or Webster County. No one was ever charged in the case or even a suspect named. Just like Ben Walker, Walter Permenter was to become another forgotten victim of this tragic case.

It had been more than two years since Janie Sharp's murder. Cases had been prepared, arrangements had been made and there was little desire by either party to delay the trial for any extended period of time. After a one-week delay, the final trial of Ernest Swinton Permenter would take place on August 12, 1912.

9. THE JUDGE

George Alonzo McLean fit the stereotype as a Southern circuit riding judge of the early 20th century. Born in 1859 to a genteel slaveholding family, George slept with a companion slave boy at the foot of his bed until the end of the Civil War.

McLean studied law and served a term in the Mississippi Senate before settling into a life as a circuit judge in the 5th District of Mississippi. This District encompassed six counties including Winston. His duties required holding court sessions twice a year in each county.

He had four children with his first wife who died from complications giving birth at a young age. A few years later he remarried and had two additional children. The youngest was George Alonzo McLean, Jr who achieved success as the owner/publisher of The Tupelo Daily Journal and a community activist. The younger McLean is the subject of the book: *Tupelo Man – the Life and Times of George McLean, a Most Peculiar Newspaper Publisher by Robert Blade*. Much of the information concerning Judge McLean was derived from this book.

The McLean household in Winona was a boisterous one and the Judge wasn't involved in the day to day activities of his children until a situation dictated that a stern Presbyterian hand be applied.

McLean was a major landowner and controlled as much as ten thousand acres of farmland at one time. He was an early automobile enthusiast and drove a Model T to range about the countryside and inspect his properties. He once took the family on a trip across the West reaching as far as Pike's Peak in a Franklin Touring car.

The Judge was tall, lean and proper and well respected by his peers. The Supreme Court ruling that overturned the conviction in the first trial of Swinton Permenter likely was a bitter pill for him to swallow. He now had every intention of conducting a procedurally proper and well-disciplined second trial. The publicity surrounding the case would demand it. The legal profession, every politician and every newspaper in the state of Mississippi and many across the country had all eyes upon this trial.

The prosecution recognized the gravity of the case as well and the area District Attorney T. L. Lamb of Eupora was assisted by as many as six additional counsels including the Montgomery County Attorney Wellborn, W.S. Knox of Winona, the former District Attorney Rueben Jones and his son, H.F. Jones of Louisville, J. A. Teat of Kosciusko and ex-Congressman Shed Hill. Hill took the lead on much of the questioning during the trial.

Not to be outdone, the defense gathered as many as six attorneys. Swinton Permenter's original legal team from the first trial consisting of H.H. Rodgers, L.H. Hopkins and Z.A. Brantley was still intact. Local attorneys, Witty and Thompson were added as a late addition and the lead attorney was a well-known barrister from Hazelhurst named R.N. Miller. After the trial began, a former district attorney from the 6th District and now a practicing attorney in Memphis, J.B. Webb, joined the defense team.

*****

The little town of Winona in central Mississippi would be the center of attention of the entire state and much of the nation over the next 12 days as newspaper reporters and members of the legal profession crowded into the area. Winona was a well-established community nestled in the hills just to the east of the fertile Mississippi Delta.

The county courthouse was well suited for such a major trial. Located in the center of town, the elaborate structure was almost new - built in 1904. It was demolished in the mid-1970's and the city library has since been erected on the spot. All that remains today is a confederate monument that bears a striking resemblance to the monument located in the center of Louisville and a monument stone denoting the date of construction.

Winona was significantly larger than Louisville at that time. The population of twenty-five hundred was fed by the intersection of two railroads and its proximity to the vast farmlands of the Delta. Much like Natchez, another more famous city farther to the south, Winona benefitted when more affluent landowners chose to live in the nearby hill communities believing that it was a healthier environment with fewer mosquitos and diseases.

Winona had continued to prosper in spite of a yellow fever epidemic that decimated the population in 1878 and a fire, ten years later that destroyed the downtown business district.

In an interesting side note, Winona suffered through its own tragic murder case in the 1990's when the owner and three employees of the downtown Tardy Furniture Company were brutally murdered. It took six trials and numerous Supreme Court rulings before the accused was convicted and sentenced to death.

*****

There is no longer an official transcript of the second Swinton Permenter trial. Too many years have passed and too many custodians of these documents have come and gone. But the sensational nature of this case piqued the interest of newspapers across the country. One paper, The Commercial Appeal in Memphis took a special interest and covered the case from beginning to end with special daily reports from the courtroom. These newspaper reports provided details of testimony and conflicts throughout the trial and are the basis for the following chapters.

The trial opened on Monday, August 12, 1912 in the courtroom of the Montgomery County Courthouse. The heat was oppressive as to be expected in Mississippi in August but it had little or no impact on the size of the crowd that had gathered to watch this legal battle. The courtroom and gallery were packed and there were even a few ladies in the audience which was extremely rare in rural Mississippi in the early 1900's. In spite of the heat and the size of the crowd, good order was maintained throughout the trial. The only real interruption in the proceedings occurred when Judge McLean ordered bailiffs to find and install electric fans at times to cool witnesses and sometimes members of the audience.

Judge McLean opened court proceedings at 2:00 pm, the hottest time of the day. After each side announced their readiness to continue, jury selection began. One hundred possible jurors had received summons and were on hand to be questioned by the prosecution and defense teams. Men were brought to the jury box in groups of twelve– this man eliminated for this bias, another eliminated for a connection to someone associated with the case, yet another not considered for some perceived prejudice. It was 7:00 pm when the court was adjourned for the night. Only six jurors had been selected out of the first fifty interviewed.

Taking extra caution, Judge McLean had arranged for four special bailiffs to assist with the case and to care for and monitor the jurors. The six jurors selected were instructed demonstratively to not discuss the case among themselves in any form and the bailiffs were instructed to not allow anyone to approach them.

Jury selection began again on Tuesday morning and it took until the noon break to seat a full jury of twelve men. These men were of Montgomery County and had no known connections to the case or the families involved. Interestingly enough, all were listed as farmers. According to the Commercial Appeal, they ranged from the age of 24 to 45 and most were family men. The jury is listed as follows:

J.R. Bennett, J.F. Castles, M.H. Ferguson, G.C. Ingram, W.D Loweriman, J.T. Mann, T. H. Moore (referred to later as C.L. Moore), Fred Parker, E.M. Stephens, L. H. Sykes, J.G Taylor and J.W. Tinnon

Testimony would begin after lunch at 1:00 pm and if it was possible the courtroom was more crowded than on Monday. According to the Commercial Appeal – *"a surging crowd of humanity filled every available space in the courtroom, and so oppressive did it become that Judge McLean dispatched bailiffs for fans for the jury, attorneys and some of the spectators."*

10. NEW TRIAL OPENS

TUESDAY, AUGUST 13, 1912

Testimony began after the lunch break as the prosecution presented its case. Martha E. Sharp, the mother of Janie Sharp was the first to testify. Mrs. Sharp was dressed in black from head to toe to convey that she was still in mourning for her daughter. She was composed throughout her testimony. The District Attorney began by asking Mrs. Sharp to relay the incidents of the day of the murder.

Martha Sharp testified that Miss Janie had helped her clean away the dishes from the noon meal and had decided to take the one and a half mile walk from their home to the post office and stores in Rural Hill. She intended to pick up the family's mail and make some purchases of sewing needs.

At this point, the handkerchief found in Swinton Permenter's pocket was admitted into evidence. Mrs. Sharp was asked to identify it. She was at first uncertain until Prosecutor Teal provided his glasses for her use. Upon donning the spectacles, she identified it as Janie's noting a small tear in one corner of the cloth.

Mrs. Sharp continued to testify indicating that she became concerned when Janie did not return home by late in the day and went in search of her daughter. Mrs. Sharp indicated that Janie would have traveled along the Commodore Road and that there were no houses directly on the road for her to pass. To her knowledge, Janie had not been seen along the road.

In cross examination, Defense Attorney Miller attempted to question Mrs. Sharp's identification of the handkerchief. She was unwavering in her certainty stating that it was the same one that Janie had on the day of the murder. When asked how she could be certain, she stated that it was a highly prized gift from Janie's grandmother and had been given to her a year before her death.

Apparently Miller continued to question and badger Mrs. Sharp about the handkerchief until Judge McLean intervened and instructed the defense to move on.

When asked about the Permenter family, Mrs. Sharp noted that they were neighbors on good terms prior to the murder. She was adamant that there was no courting relationship between Swinton and her daughter, Janie.

Several witnesses who had seen Janie that day were then called by the prosecution.

Oscar McWhorter testified that he was at Rural Hill that afternoon and had seen Janie. He had left his home around noon that day with a wagon to be loaded with an engine. He stated that he was standing by his loaded wagon when Janie came out of Williams' store. He noted that she had a parasol and some bundles in her hand as she left. He was not certain of the time but he did hear the store clock strike three as he pulled away from Rural Hill.

In cross examination, Defense Attorney Miller questioned the legitimacy of McWhorter's testimony and asked if he had previously read his testimony over from the previous trial. McWhorter admitted that someone had read it to him from the record as he wanted to refresh his memory.

The next witness was Yancey Lowery. Lowery's wife was a cousin of Swinton Permenter. He was also in Rural Hill that afternoon and had seen Janie at the store. He remained at the store after Janie left and believed that the store clock struck three about fifteen or twenty minutes after Janie left.

Under cross examination, Lowery was asked if he had seen a handkerchief in Janie's hand while at the store. He indicated that he had but could not identify it or determine if it had been freshly laundered.

The store owner, Dill (later referred to as Josh) Williams was the next to testify. He recalled that Janie had been at the store sometime after dinner (in the South, the noon day meal is often referred to as dinner) but he could not say the exact time. He did remember selling yarn and spool thread and wrapping them in separate packages for Janie. He apparently did not have the trimmings that Janie was looking for and she left to go to the other store in Rural Hill, Shumach's. She did not find the items there and returned to his store before she left Rural Hill. He also stated that she indicated that she would be going to the Cyrus Ray home when she left Rural Hill. (The Cyrus Ray home was located down a side road off the Commodore Road.)

Three other witnesses testified that they had also seen Janie that day. Van Schemata said he was near the store and saw Janie leave about the time that the store clock struck three. Miss Lois Schumacher also claimed to see Janie that day with her bundles and parasol.

Bessie Ray was the last witness of the day. She was not specifically identified but investigation reveals that she was a young woman of approximately the same age as Janie and Swinton Permenter and likely a cousin of Janie's. Her testimony was limited to the handkerchief. When handed to her, she positively identified it as the one belonging to Janie.

As the first day of testimony closed, it became apparent that much of the case would hinge upon the handkerchief. If the jury believed it to be Janie's without a reasonable doubt it would be difficult for the defense team to explain.

WEDNESDAY, AUGUST 14, 1912

Court resumed at 8:30 am with more witnesses concerning Janie's presence at Rural Hill and the time frame. John Holden testified that he was as Rural Hill at the time of the mail delivery – around 1:00 pm and remained there for a period of time. He did not recall seeing Janie. Under cross examination, he indicated that he spent time at Shumach's store and did not see her there are at the William's store during that time.

Claude Massey was the next to testify. His recollection was that he actually met Janie on the Commodore Road about a quarter mile from Rural Hill after she left. Defense Attorney Rogers asked if Massey had seen anyone else on the road that afternoon. He denied seeing anyone. Rogers then created a small stir in the courtroom when he asked, "Didn't you tell Church Edwards at the Hinze Post Office that you saw Hewlett Ray and Tom McElroy on the Commodore Road that evening?

Massey replied, "No sir, I did not!"

After Massey left the stand, a map was submitted into evidence. A former sheriff of Winston County, J.W. Gully, had made a map of the Commodore Road and the paths apparently traveled by Janie on the day of the murder. This was submitted for the jury to examine.

The next witness called would spend five hours on the stand. Lee

Sharp was Janie's older brother and was convinced of Swinton Permenter's guilt from the beginning as his testimony would indicate.

Lee spoke of the search for his sister on Thursday evening, July 21, 1910. He stated that he and a group of men from the community were searching along Commodore Road and entered a strip of woods on the east side of the road. It was here that they saw Swinton for the first time that evening around 10:00 pm. Lee stated that Swinton was alone and on foot and upon approaching the party of men, he lay down by a small tree. Lee told Permenter that Janie had disappeared and they were out looking for her and feared the worst. Permenter stated that he didn't know where she was but "a nigger might have done it." Lee indicated that he saw a pistol in Permenter's pocket at that time.

The men continued to search; some wanted to search farther north but Lee suggested that they go further east. They came upon some thick brush and prepared to search it when Permenter said, "Boys, it's no use going in there. I've hunted those woods thoroughly." Lee wanted to search in the underbrush but for some reason did not at that time.

Sharp stated that as the moon had gone down, some of the men lit torches and continued the search over a large area of fields and woods. Permenter stayed with them throughout the search. As the party reached an area northwest of Rural Hill, Lee stated that Permenter made a strange statement.

"Let's go look on yonder way" pointing in a direction opposite of where Janie's body was eventually found. Putting his hand over his breast, Permenter then said, "Something in here tells me she's back that way."

Sharp indicated that they continued to search until the early morning hours before deciding to break for daylight. He returned to the search prior to everyone else at around 6:00 am. Lee began his search not far from the Sharp home as he scanned the west side of the Commodore Road. He entered a small ravine that led to a branch. It was here that he found the body of his sister.

Lee Sharp testified that Janie's body was lying flat in the branch partially submerged in the water with one leg sticking out. He saw that her throat had been cut half way around and there was a "powerful bruise" on her head as if done by a pistol butt. Between her legs lay her parasol and on her left side lay the bundles from the store. Sharp testified that he did not move her body and that he shrieked several times for help.

Sharp also testified that after Janie's funeral on Saturday, he returned to the scene and began searching for clues. He observed tracks coming from the Commodore Road that appeared to be those of a man and woman and a spot where it appeared that a scuffle took place. The tracks continued on and the signs of another scuffle were observed. Sharp noted that they were far apart as if the parties were running. He also indicated that these tracks were about 200 yards from the Sharp home.

The prosecution now directed questioning towards Permenter's behavior and dress at the time of the murder. Sharp indicated that as Janie's body was moved to the Sharp home, Permenter was heard to say, "Well, I'll have to go home and change my clothes. Would have been here last night but I was feeling bad."

When asked what clothes Swinton Permenter was wearing on the night of the search, Lee indicated a suit of blue serge and that he had that same suit on the next morning.

At this time the court broke for lunch till 2:00 pm when Sharp resumed his testimony. The courtroom continued to be packed as the crowd suffered through the heat, not wanting to miss a single word of the trial.

The prosecution opened in the afternoon by submitting a pair of shoes belonging to the suspect. These shoes were described as low quarter shoes. (Low quarter shoes are shoes where the upper does not extend above the bony projection of the ankle) One of the shoes submitted had a hole in the sole. Sharp identified them as the shoes worn by Permenter on the night of the search.

At this point, the defense submitted a second pair of high quarter shoes as the ones worn by Permenter.

Based upon the question of the shoes, the ex-Sheriff A. P. Hull was called as a witness for the prosecution. He identified the high quarter shoes as the ones he received from his deputy along with clothing belonging to the defendant. He noted that they were wet when he received them. He also identified the handkerchief as the one provided to him by the deputy.

W. R. Hull, the former deputy who collected the clothes from the Permenter home, identified the clothing and shoes and indicated that he had actually taken them to the jail in Winona and Permenter had identified them as his property.

The witch-hazel stick that had been cut at the scene of the crime to measure the footprints was then submitted into evidence. When compared to the high quarter shoes, the stick did not match the shoe size.

Before the conclusion of that day's proceedings, testimony was provided by Cyrus Ray. Little is known about this and was not directly referred to in newspaper reports. It seemed to have no direct bearing on the case.

11. SUSPICIOUS BEHAVIOR

THURSDAY, AUGUST 15, 1912

As the trial resumed, Mrs. Permenter, the mother of Swinton, sat by his side for the first time. She was dressed in traditional black much like Mrs. Sharp on the first day of testimony although Mrs. Permenter had a more recent cause for her mourning due to the recent murder of her oldest son, Walter.

As if to counter the impact of Permenter's mother at his side, Janie's father, W. C. Sharp was in the courtroom for the first time since the trial started. According to reports, Mr. Sharp's physical condition had greatly deteriorated and was most likely affected by the strain and stress of having to deal with the murder of his daughter and the uncertainty of the trial.

The courtroom was again packed with a full gallery and the heat was oppressive. The day's first witness was a young man named Forrest Ray. He was initially questioned by Prosecution Attorney Treat. His testimony indicated that on the day of the murder he had been at his home which was actually on the Sharp family's place. Later that day he went to the home of his uncle, Benton Ray and here he saw Earl Ray and his sister, Nessie. Later on that day between 4 and 5 o'clock, he went to a field that was near the Commodore Road with a gentleman by the name of Nathan Sharp and from there he went to the home of another uncle, Cyrus Ray.

It was here that he heard Cyrus Ray's daughter say, "You all had better be hunting for Janie. I just learned a little while ago she's missing and can't be found."

Forrest Ray indicated that this was the first time he knew anything of Janie Sharp missing. He testified that he first went to the Sharp home and then started toward Rural Hill. Along the way, he met Janie's Father.

At Mr. Sharp's request, Forrest Ray had searched along the Commodore Road to see if he could find any of Janie's tracks. He indicated that he did observe some tracks of a woman. From there he went back toward his uncle's home (Cyrus Ray) and while in the woods he saw several more tracks. The sight of the woman's tracks concerned him and he went on to his uncle's house and got a horse and with others rode to the home of O. L. Permenter. O.L. was an uncle of Swinton and his home was nearly a mile from that of Cyrus Ray's. Forrest Ray asked O. L. if he had seen any sign of Miss Janie and he replied that he had not. At this point, Ray and the group of men with him went back to the Commodore Road.

When they got back to the road they found that a crowd of people had begun to gather to discuss and help with the search for Janie. They tied their horses and began to assist on foot in the search. Forrest Ray indicated that he first saw Swinton Permenter on the night of the search at around 10 p.m. He did state that he had been to the Permenter's house earlier and that he had not found Swinton there. He indicated that later that night, Permenter was with the party of searchers that included Lee Sharp as he had previously testified.

Forrest Ray also corroborated Lee Sharp's testimony about Permenter's statements concerning his search of the patch of woods.

The next witness that day was a man by the name of Earl Ray (reported as the fiancée of Janie) who lived only a quarter of a mile from the Sharp place at that time. His testimony corroborated much of what Forrest Ray had said. He indicated that he was at home with his sisters till about 5:00 p.m. on the day of the murder. He then went to a field near Commodore Road and from there to his Uncle Cyrus Ray's home. Just like the previous witness, he testified that this was where he learned that Janie was missing.

From there he went to the Commodore Road to join in the search. Shortly before sunset, Earl Ray along with a man by the name of Tom McCool went to Ed Permenter's home and asked if anyone had seen Janie. Swinton was not there at the time. They went back to the Commodore Road and joined the crowd but later returned for a second time to the Permenter home about dark and asked the family if Swinton was there. They were again told that Swinton was not there. Earl Ray stated that he later saw Swinton sometime between 10 and 11 o'clock that night on the road but did not hear the remarks that others claimed were made by Swinton. He noted that Swinton was present the next morning when Janie's body was found and that he acted somewhat strangely and sat about 15 to 20 feet away from the crowd and lay down there at a small tree.

When cross-examined by the defense, Earl Ray admitted that he had interest in Miss Janie prior to her death and that there was another young man named Whitmire who also had interest in her as well. He acknowledged that he had been the fiancée of Miss Janie and that they had been engaged for more than a year. He also said that he had been at the Sharp home on the Sunday before the murder on the following Thursday.

The next prosecution witness was Hewlett Ray, one of the men accused by Ben Walker. He testified that on the day of the murder he was working on the farm that he had rented from Tom McElroy. Late in the afternoon when he learned that Jamie had disappeared he left his work chopping cotton in the field and later that evening went to the Permenter home with William and Forrest Ray - arriving there around 9 p.m. but saw no one there. They got with a search party and later saw Swinton Permenter on the Commodore Road. Hewlett Ray corroborated the testimony by Lee Sharp and others that Permenter seemed to discourage the party to search certain parts of the woods.

Under cross-examination by the Defense Attorney Miller, Hewlett Ray was asked if he had been informed that the detective Ben Walker was out and about hunting for people who may have killed Janie Sharp. He claimed he had not been aware of that. Defense Attorney Miller said "Didn't you tell Walker to let you and your business alone and if he did not you would make it interesting for him?"

"No sir, I did not say any such thing."

When accused by the defense, he positively denied using foul language and brandishing a pistol in the crowd that next morning when Miss Janie's body was found.

Tom McElroy was the next witness. This caused a stir in the courtroom crowd as McElroy along with Hewlett Ray had temporarily been arrested in the case. In his testimony he stated that at the time of Janie's murder he was living about a mile and one half from the Sharp home. On that day he was at home with his father-in-law and mother-in-law. He noted that he received information that Janie was missing about sundown and he immediately went toward the Sharp home and along the way he met a group of men who were hunting for her. McElroy indicated that they were all on the Commodore Road between 8 and 9 o'clock and he noted that like the others, he saw Swinton Permenter in the crowd at around 10 p.m. He also said that the last time he has seen Janie before her death was about two weeks prior.

Defense attorneys took the opportunity to ask him what shoe size he wore and he indicated that he wore a size nine. Under cross-examination he also denied having heard Hewlett Ray say that if Janie was found her throat would be cut. When asked, he informed the court that he sold his farm the following September in 1910 and moved to Texas in an effort to try to provide better for his family and himself. Defense Counsel Miller then asked if an affidavit had been made out against him for the murder of Janie Sharp. The prosecution counsel Hill objected but then withdrew his objection and McElroy was instructed to answer. He said yes, an affidavit had been made against him.

When the prosecution was able to redirect, McElroy was asked about the outcome of the affidavit. There was an objection by the defense but after some discussion, Judge McClain overruled the objection and the witness indicated that the affidavit had been dismissed without prosecution.

The long day of testimony continued throughout with a parade of witnesses. The prosecution's next witness was Tom McCool. During his testimony he indicated that he reached the vicinity of the murder as darkness approached and joined in the search. At some point, he went to the Ed Permenter home to see if Swinton was there but did not find him. As he returned back along Commodore Road, he met Swinton and his uncle O. L. Permenter about a half mile from his home sometime between 9:00 and 10:00 pm.

McCool asked Permenter, "Why ain't you not assisting in the search for Janie?"

He stated that Swinton replied, "Well, wait until I go home and get a horse to ride and I'll go with you."

McCool responded, "There's no use getting a horse. I am walking and so can you."

McCool's testimony indicated that Swinton consented to join him but implied that it took some persuasion on his part. As they walked along the road, the men heard a dog bark in the nearby woods and McCool said to Permenter: "I'll bet that dog is barking where Miss Janie's body is lying."

McCool indicated that Permenter responded, "Oh, it ain't nothing but a dead possum and it ain't no use for us to go in there."

McCool believed that Janie's body was found the next morning about 200 yards from where he first met Permenter on the road that night.

The next witness for the prosecution was a man named Davis Steed. Steed lived in nearby Attala County but near the Hinze Post Office located south of Rural Hill. His testimony centered around a previous statement made by Swinton Permenter.

Steed testified that on a Saturday evening about two weeks before the murder, he attended a prayer meeting at the Horn schoolhouse and happened to be sitting beside Swinton. They began whispering about some of the local girls and that he remarked that two of the girls in attendance that night were about the prettiest girls he had ever seen in his life.

He indicated that Swinton responded by referring to Janie Sharp and said he would give ten dollars and be willing to spend ten years of his life in jail to receive the affection of Janie.

The defense counsel questioned Steed about the statement and asked if he had been paid (hired) to make such a statement. Steed answered by emphatically denying the accusation.

The next witness was Dr. W. M. Clemmons, the dentist who lived near Rural Hill not far from the Williams' store. Clemmons testimony was straightforward. Clemmons said that he remembered the day well and upon hearing of Miss Janie's disappearance through a personal message he went to aid in the search. Not far from Rural Hill, he met a group of men and joined them. At some point he left the group and went in search of the local Methodist minister named T. L. Oaks. Clemmons thought that perhaps Janie had eloped and married some young man in the community. After searching, he was not able to find the clergyman.

He later went to the home of O.L. Permenter with two other men in hopes of finding Swinton there and that he might have some information but was not successful.

The next morning, he heard shouting on the Commodore Road and went the spot where Janie's body was found. A Justice of the Peace named McAlilly was on the scene and because of his medical background, McAlilly requested that Clemmons examine the body. Clemmons approached Janie's corpse along with two other men and determined that she was indeed deceased and he described the position of the body and the nature of her wounds.

In the last part of his testimony, Clemmons shook the defense when he stated that he had heard Swinton remark that if old man Sharp (Janie's father) didn't mind he would be sorry for it someday. Clemmons believed the remark was made because Will Sharp had forbid Permenter from visiting his home.

The next prosecution witness seemed to catch the prosecution off guard when under cross examination, Will Gladney acknowledged that Hewlett Ray (another of the men "arrested" by Ben Walker) had carried a shotgun during the search for Janie and had cursed and swore when her body was found. He also stated that Hewlett Ray remarked that if suspicions against Permenter got much stronger he would shoot his damn brains out. This was in direct conflict with Hewlett Ray's testimony given earlier in the day.

The final witness of the day was Newt McCool and his statements centered around the search for Swinton Permenter on the night of the search. His testimony corroborated earlier testimony as he was also sent to O.L. Permenter's home by Will Sharp to ask about Swinton but could not find him.

12. PROSECUTION RESTS

FRIDAY, AUGUST 16, 1912

Court reconvened on Friday at 8:30 am with a still packed courtroom and Swinton's mother still by his side as she sat stone faced throughout the testimony. Will Sharp, Janie's father was also in the courtroom in spite of the fact that he had become ill during the previous day.

The prosecution's next witness was John Edwards. Edwards had been on the scene when Janie's body was found. His testimony indicated that Swinton Permenter was there as well and as talk circulated that bloodhounds would certainly be brought in to track the killer, he heard Swinton remark that if dogs were brought into the search, they would certainly track him as he had been in those woods the night before searching for Janie.

When cross examined, Edwards admitted that he had been convicted of carrying a concealed weapon in the past but also stated that he had no bad feelings toward Swinton or his family.

Webster Schumacher also testified that he heard Permenter make the same remark. When asked by the defense if he thought that the comment may have been made in jest, Schumacher indicated that he didn't think so.

The next witness, Josh McGee also testified to the statement made by Permenter. The defense team asked McGee if Permenter looked or acted peculiar throughout this time but the witness said he didn't really pay attention to that. It was noted in his testimony that it had been raining and that he had loaned his raincoat to cover Janie's body.

The next major witness was not present in the courtroom. The reason that Terrell Hall did not appear was not stated in the newspaper report but both sides agreed to have his written testimony read into the record. Prosecutor Teal read to the jury:

Hall was at the Will Sharp home at around 9:00 am on the morning that Janie's body had been brought there. He was in the company of Swinton Permenter and asked Swinton if he could borrow a coat. They left the Sharp home and walked to Permenter's home. Hall testified that he did not go inside but stood by the front gate. A few minutes passed and he saw Swinton come out to the porch with a wash pan, enter a right hand side room of the house where he washed and changed clothes. He noted that Permenter had on a blue colored suit at first but came out in a different set of clothing. Swinton and other members of his family went back to the Sharp home riding in a wagon while Hall and Swinton's father walked the short distance. Later Hall walked back to the Permenter home with Mr. Permenter.

His written statement indicated that later, he went into the side room where Swinton had bathed and changed and found the clothes he had been previously wearing. He stated that in the pants pocket was a Barlow knife, a plug of tobacco and two handkerchiefs – one belonging to a man and the other was obviously a lady's handkerchief. He indicated that the lady's handkerchief was smaller and had figures around the border.

It was never stated in the testimony why he felt the need to examine Swinton's clothing.

J. T. Hanna was the next to testify for the prosecution. Hanna was the owner and handler of the bloodhound used that day. Hanna testified that he had trained dogs all of his life as had his father and grandfather before him. The dog was a registered bloodhound named Ruth Hindoo and while she was only fourteen months old, she had proven her ability to track.

Hanna started the dog at the branch where Janie's body was found. According to his testimony the dog ran north along the branch for forty yards where the dog struck a hole of water and scented on top of the water. The dog then went down the east side of the branch and he noticed what appeared to be scuffling places on the ground. The dog then tracked in a southeasterly direction and not much farther, he noticed tracks that appeared to be made by a man and a woman. A few feet further down the branch, he observed a mule track. Tracking further, the dog struck a small ravine and followed it up to an old road where a man's track was seen. The dog crossed the road and entered a nearby crossroad where Hanna saw more tracks made by a man and a woman.

The dog then trailed south and headed for the Ed Permenter farm. When the dog reached the corner of the yard of the home, Hanna checked her at the gate. Someone in the crowd said, "let her go!" He released the dog who then headed to the road in front of the home and scented several men standing there before returning toward the house. The dog trailed around the home lot and the stable and barn before returning to the gate. She then angled across a nearby field of cotton before returning once again to the gate in front of the home.

It was here that Ed Permenter, Swinton's father met him and said, "Hello, Hanna, you look natural."

Hanna replied, "Yes, but I do want a drink of water."

The dog began tracking again and scented a group of five men standing nearby. Swinton Permenter was standing in the center of this group. According to Hanna, the dog looked Swinton over, scented him and through his head back.

Hanna testified that at this point he saw Walter Permenter, Swinton's older brother on the steps of the porch with what appeared to be a gun in his hand. His testimony implied that he was concerned that Walter might want to kill him or his dog.

Cyrus Ray was recalled to the stand to corroborate Hanna's testimony concerning the tracks seen near where Janie was found.

The last witness called was a man named Rueben Hunt who was in the party trailing the bloodhound. He also described the route taken by the dog.

As 5:00 pm approached, the prosecution rested its case. While a great deal of evidence was presented, most if not all was circumstantial - the very problem that led to the previous trial decision being overturned. The prosecution's case would hinge upon convincing the jury that the handkerchief was indeed the one that Janie possessed at the time of her murder and establishing that Swinton Permenter was the only individual with a desire, opportunity and motive to take her life.

The trial would continue on Saturday and now the defense would have the opportunity to present its witnesses, refute the prosecution's witnesses and cast a reasonable doubt upon the guilt of Swinton Permenter.

13. DEFENSE BEGINS

SATURDAY, AUGUST 17, 1912

The trial began again at 8:30 on Saturday morning. Before the defense began to present its case, Defense Attorney Miller made a motion to dismiss the case against his client. He asked that all evidence submitted by the prosecution be excluded and for the judge to instruct the jury to find Swinton Permenter not guilty. Judge McLean immediately overruled the motion and instructed the defense to proceed.

The defense plan was simple; to call into question the timeline of events and prove that Swinton didn't have an opportunity to commit the crime, repudiate or at least provide contradictory evidence to that provided by prosecution witnesses and to provide an explanation for the lady's handkerchief found in Permenter's clothing.

The defense's first witness was Buster Burchfield who had been at Rural Hill on the day of Janie's murder. He testified that he spoke with Josh (Dill) Williams, the owner of the store, on the following day about the time that Janie left his store at Rural Hill.

Josh (Dill) Williams was recalled by the defense and asked about the time. Williams again stated that he could not remember but he did add that Janie had paid cash for part of her purchases and had charged the rest on that day. It is uncertain from the record if Williams was unclear about the time or about the conversation he had with Burchfield.

Gus Blaine testified that he had been deputized and was one of the men sent to get the clothes from the Ed Permenter home that Swinton had been wearing previously. He stated that he found the clothes and two handkerchiefs in a coat. Under cross-examination by the prosecution, Blaine said that he couldn't remember stating in the first trial that he had told District Attorney Lamb that he found the handkerchiefs in a pants pocket.

Hugh Hobby was a young boy at the time of the murder, age thirteen. He was called as the next witness. His testimony was that he had been swimming with his two brothers in Lobutcha Creek not far from the Hinze Post Office. (The community of Hinze is located a short distance (roughly three and one half miles) from Rural Hill just southeast and across Lobutcha Creek.) He indicated that they arrived at the swimming hole around 2:00 pm and had passed the mail rider along the way.

When the Hobby boys reached the swimming hole, they found Swinton Permenter, Lon Burchfield, Levi Burchfield and Ezra Brazest already there. (Brazest was probably Brazeal or Breazeale. Brazeal will be used here as it was most commonly referred to in testimony). A short time later, they all left the creek together and headed back toward the Hinze Post Office. Hobby testified that along the way, Alonzo Burchfield stated that he had to get back to the field and his plowing. Permenter replied. "it ain't work time yet." Ezra Brazeal pulled his watch out of his pocket and noted that it was 2:25 pm.

Alonzo (Lon) Burchfield who was swimming with Swinton was the next to testify. He indicated that Swinton approached him (likely while he was plowing) around noon and asked him to go to the swimming hole with him. They stopped at the Hinze Post Office for as much as an hour while Swinton conducted some business there. While not indicated in the trial report, it had been stated that Permenter was arranging for the purchase and delivery of several bottles of wine. From there the young men went to the pool and stayed for roughly an hour. Burchfield indicated that they did not pass the mail rider along the way. He also recalled the conversation about the time as they were returning to the Hinze Post Office and that according to Brazeal's watch it was 2:35 pm.

Burchfield then testified that he, Levi Burchfield and Swinton crossed the field he had been plowing and went to the Burchfield house where Levi drew some water for them to drink. He did not know the exact time but in his opinion it was about 3:20 pm. He then stated that Swinton went with him back toward the field where he was working and they separated at the nearby crossroads. He estimated the time to be 3:30 pm.

Under cross-examination, Burchfield denied hearing Swinton says, "Do you think a man could have plowed all this land from 3:20 till sundown?" (this referenced the field that Burchfield had been plowing and the statement had been attributed to Permenter by others).

He also denied making a statement to Walter Cummins that he knew Permenter was guilty and that Permenter had asked him to help move Miss Janie's body to the creek.

Walter Bennett, the mail rider was the next defense witness. Bennett rode the "Star" route from the Vowell Community to Rural Hill. He indicated that the normal schedule was followed that day which included delivery at Rural Hill around noon and leaving that community at around 1:00 pm. He normally arrived at the Hinze Post Office at 2:10 pm. He stated that along the route he did hear a group of young boys shouting and playing at the swimming hole but that it was as much as 200 yards from the road so he did not see who might have been there. He did meet his uncle and a man named Tom Gregory along the way but they walked ahead as he stopped to water his horse. He looked at his watch as he stopped and noted that it was 2:16 pm. Bennett could not remember passing the Hobby boys along his route.

Several more witnesses were called to confirm the defense's timeline. Medder Hobby, the brother of Hugh, testified that Brazeal's watch indicated 2:35 pm as the group returned to Hinze Post Office. Ezra Brazeal testified that his watch indicated 2:35 pm as well.

The last witness of the day was the mother of Alonzo and Levi Burchfield. Mrs. George Burchfield testified that she had seen Swinton Permenter on the day of Janie's murder for the first time between 12:00 and 1:00 pm. She indicated that her two sons went with Swinton to the swimming hole and that they returned at around 3:20 pm that afternoon.

The defense had been effective in establishing a time line of Swinton Permenter's activities until roughly 3:30 pm on the day of the murder. If the testimony was believed, it would establish that Swinton had been as much as two miles away from the scene of the murder at or near the time that Janie was last seen around 3:00 pm as she left Rural Hill.

The Saturday session of court adjourned early at 4:00 pm. Testimony would resume on Monday.

14. TIMELINE

SUNDAY, AUGUST 18,1912

The court was in recess for the Sabbath. The jury was under the watchful eyes of two bailiffs charged with their care. Jury members were not allowed to attend church but they did have the opportunity to stroll about the little town of Winona for a little fresh air and some exercise.

A special report in the Commercial Appeal indicated that the defense planned to call witnesses till at least Wednesday. Considering rebuttals and closing arguments, the case would not likely go to the jury before the next Friday.

MONDAY & TUESDAY, AUGUST 18, 19, 1912

Court convened again at 8:30 am as the defense called its next witness, Dillard Vowell. Dillard was the son of Elbert Vowell who figured so strongly in the case of Ben Walker. The Vowells were relatives of the Permenter family. Dillard confirmed the time frame given by the previous defense witnesses. He related leaving the swimming hole on Lobutcha Creek with the Burchfields, the Hobbys and Swinton Permenter and noted the time given by Ezra

Brazeal as 2:35 pm.

The next witness was George Burchfield, the father of Lon and Levi, the boys who had been with Swinton that day. His testimony supported the timeline given by the previous defense witnesses. Under cross-examination by Prosecutor Hill, he denied making a statement to two men, D.R. Dempsey and John Ray that he saw Swinton leave his place at 2:20 not 3:30 as he stated. This statement was supposedly made on the road to Louisville just prior to first trial.

Burchfield's other son Levi was the next on the stand and he corroborated the other witnesses in reference to the timeframe.

The postmaster and owner of the store in the Hinze community was also called to testify. In his statement, he noted that it was about a quarter of a mile from the store/post office to the swimming hole. He remembered that the boys in the group left the post office sometime before the mail rider arrived from Rural Hill. He was not required to keep written records of the arrival and departure of the mail rider so he could not be exact in his timeline but did recall that he saw Lon Burchfield and Swinton Permenter return from the swimming hole.

The parade of witnesses continued throughout the next two days and included several of Permenter's relatives. Next on the stand was Swinton's sister Nellie. At the time of the trial, Nellie was twenty-five and was living with her parents at the time of the murder. Nellie stated that on the morning of that day, her father was plowing in a nearby field and by late morning, her mother had left to go to Mr. Schumacher's store in Hinze. She didn't want to stay at home alone so around noon she decided to visit her sister who was married to a man named Tom Gregory. The Gregory's lived a short distance away. She indicated that Swinton left the house shortly before her and was headed to the swimming hole at

Lobutcha Creek to meet the Burchfield boys. She stopped at the Burchfield's nearby home before passing the mailbox and going to the Gregory's. She saw her father plowing in the field along the way. Later in the day she saw Swinton returning past the Gregory house toward home. She noted the time as 3:45pm as she was concerned that he should have been plowing. She returned home 20-30 minutes later and saw Swinton plowing in a field across a small branch.

Nellie claimed that she was outside much of the afternoon potting flowers in the yard and observed Swinton several times throughout the afternoon. At one point, Nellie indicated that Swinton met with his father and exchanged horses and her father left to go to the blacksmith shop to get his plow sharpened. While the horses were being swapped, she was with Swinton as they ate some apples on the edge of the yard. She couldn't provide the exact time but noted that it was late afternoon. Swinton then returned to the field and continued plowing till sundown.

Nellie stated that late that afternoon she had spoken with a group of negroes who were living on the Sharp's farm and they informed her that Janie was missing. She indicated that she was the first person to inform Swinton of Janie's disappearance. Her mother had been informed while at the home of O.L. Permenter, Swinton's uncle.

While Nellie was talking to Swinton, the phone rang and their cousin, Lemander Vowell, talked to Swinton and informed him that help was needed in the search. Nellie indicated that Swinton left after supper – just before dark and that she did not see him again until 3:00 am the next morning. Later, Bob McCool and Tom Ray had been to the Permenter home and asked for Swinton and if she knew that Janie was missing.

Nellie was then asked about Swinton's clothing. When Swinton left that evening he was wearing a blue serge coat and a blue checked linen colored shirt. She indicated that when he came home later the next morning, he changed clothes because he had gotten wet during the search. Nellie indicated that she was not at home when the sheriff's officers arrived to get Swinton's clothes.

Nellie was questioned about the handkerchief that was submitted into evidence and had the following to tell the court: Nellie and many in the community had attended a July 4th picnic at Indian Springs in 1910 prior to the murder. Her now deceased older brother, Walter, found a handkerchief in his buggy while there. He gave the handkerchief to Nellie and told her to tell Swinton to find the owner. Nellie remembered that a young man named Fletcher Whitney (possible Whitmire) and Janie Sharp had been sitting in Walter's buggy alongside another buggy with Estelle Ray and Bob McCool.

Defense Attorney Miller handed Nellie Permenter the handkerchief submitted into evidence and pulled another handkerchief from his pocket and asked her to examine them both. Nellie indicated that there was no difference between them. Miller then submitted both handkerchiefs to the jury for them to examine.

Building on the doubt created by Nellie's testimony about the handkerchief, the defense called J. L. Wilson to the stand. Wilson was at the Sharp home when Janie's body was brought there and placed on a bed. Wilson testified that he saw some bundles, a parasol and a lady's handkerchief either by or on the bed with Janie's body. Wilson claimed that a young woman named Maggie Morgan was present as well and had remarked that the handkerchief was the one belonging to Janie.

When he was cross-examined by the prosecution, Wilson indicated that there were several people in the room at the time and that others had heard Morgan make the comment but he failed to identify anyone else who could validate the statement. He also admitted that at the time of the murder, he was farming land owned by Ed Permenter and that he could not specifically identify the handkerchief.

The defense took a different direction when it recalled Lee Sharp, Janie's brother, to the stand and addressed a series of rumors about the case. Lee was first questioned about a statement he allegedly made to Henry Ray in a Louisville poolroom. Didn't he say that he would give Ray's wife, a young woman named Effie Permenter Ray and a cousin to Swinton, $100 if she would tell that she saw Swinton kill Janie. Lee Sharp denied making the offer but did admit that he told Ray that he believed Effie knew about the murder and had seen the act. When he was cross-examined by the prosecution, Sharp indicated that it was actually Ray who first made the statement – "I believe Effie knows all about the murder." Sharp indicated that he then replied, "I do too. I wish she would tell it."

Sharp was then asked if he provided a statement to The Commercial Appeal after the first trial in Louisville about a rumor that Effie Permenter (unmarried at the time of the murder) had actually witnessed Swinton commit the crime while she was washing near her father's home. Lee provided a vague answer but attributed the rumor to a Mrs. Maddox who lived near Ethel.

Judge McLean intervened at this time and specifically asked Sharp if he had any knowledge of the Detective Ben Walker and Walter Permenter searching for testimony against others that might have committed the crime. He denied any knowledge.

Henry Ray was then called as a witness and he testified that Lee Sharp did make a remark about Effie receiving $100 if she admitted what she knew about Swinton committing the murder.

Effie Permenter Ray was then called to the stand. She was fourteen at the time of the murder and denied ever telling anyone that she saw Swinton commit the crime. She claimed to have seen Swinton that afternoon around dusk.

Swinton's older sister, Mrs. Tom Gregory also claimed to have seen Swinton on the afternoon at 3:45 pm. After some discussion, Judge McLean doubted the accuracy of the time and omitted the statement from the record.

O.L. Permenter was the next witness called by the defense. O.L. was Swinton's uncle. He was also a mute and his testimony had to be interpreted by a man named J. H. Rose who knew O.L. from his time at a deaf and dumb institute as a young man. O.L. claimed to have seen Swinton plowing in a nearby field at 4:00 pm and then a later again at 4:45 pm as he returned from his brother's home (Ed Permenter) at 4:45 pm. He testified as to the accuracy of the time as he looked at a clock in his home when he stopped for a drink of water.

The last witness on the 20th was a man named Ed Owen. His testimony was immediately suspect and of little consequence. His testimony was limited to a description of tracks in the woods leading away from the location of the body. He stated that he believed the tracks belonged to a man and a woman. It is uncertain as to his testimony in the previous trial, but the newspaper reports indicated that there were some contradictions in his statement. Reports also indicated that in the previous trial, his oath was impeached on the stand.

15. SWINTON TAKES STAND

WEDNESDAY, AUGUST 20, 1912

There had been considerable speculation that Swinton Permenter would or would not testify in his own defense. That ended on Wednesday morning as Swinton was the first to take the stand. Permenter's demeanor was calm, much like it was in the first trial but his soft spoken manner proved to be a difficulty not only for the spectators but also for the stenographer, the jury and even the attorneys. He was admonished on several occasions throughout his testimony to speak up.

Led by his attorney, he began by describing himself and his relationship with Janie Sharp. He said that he was born near Rural Hill and had known Janie all of his life. He acknowledged that he had "kept company" with her as many as five or six times in the past but with other young ladies as well. He said that his interest in those of the opposite sex began at around the age of fifteen. He noted that he had visited Janie's home on half a dozen occasions over two years prior to her death. The last occasion was on the Sunday prior to her death when he spent the better part of the day there along with a group of other young people after Sunday church service at Rural Hill.

On the day of the murder, July 21, 1910, he spent the morning plowing in a field near his family's home. At around 11:30, he stopped his fieldwork and left for the Hinze Post Office at around noon in the company of the Burchfield boys with the intent of going to the swimming hole after attending to his business at the Post Office. He gave the Postmaster money to send for four quarts of sherry wine before heading to the swimming hole with the Burchfields. On the way back, he testified that Ezra Breazel had looked at his watch and noted that it was 2:36 pm. He also stated that he stopped along the way to kill a snake and a turtle.

At this point in the newspaper reports, there were some inconsistencies related to the testimony. It is possible that the reporter either misunderstood the testimony or simply made an error but it is an obvious error. The report indicated that Swinton stated that he also stopped at the store in Rural Hill to pick up a bundle of cloth for his sister who had telephoned the request to the storekeeper. This is highly unlikely. If this were true, Swinton's case would be destroyed as it would have placed him near the scene of the crime. It is likely that the store in question was located in Hinze and the reporter simply made an error.

Swinton claimed to reach the Burchfield home at 3:20, walked toward the field where the older Burchfield brother was plowing and then separated from Lon Burchfield at a fork in the road and headed home. He stopped by the house and threw the bundle of cloth through an open window onto a bed before heading back to the field to continue plowing. He plowed for roughly and hour and a half until he stopped to change horses with his father who needed to carry some plow sweeps to the blacksmith shop in Hinze to be sharpened. Swinton then stated that he returned to his fieldwork and continued plowing till sundown. A few minutes after he returned home, the telephone rang and he found out that Janie Sharp was missing.

Sometime between sunset and dark, Swinton indicated that he left home and stopped at his Uncle's home, O.L. Permenter for a period of time before meeting Tom McCool and Theo Ray on the road not far from O.L.'s house. He claimed to have asked them about the missing girl before heading to the Sharp place with McCool and Ray. From the Sharp's, they advanced to the Commodore Road and met a crowd of men involved in the search. Swinton remained with a group of men as they searched both sides of the Commodore Road until 3:00 am when the search broke up until daylight.

Swinton indicated that he started again at daylight and met other searchers near a field owned by Arthur Ray. Several of the men claimed to find tracks along the way. As part of the search, he walked through the woods when he came upon the crowd that had gathered around Janie's body. He stayed with the crowd as Janie's corpse was taken to the Sharp home. He remained there on the porch of the house for a while and then decided to go home and change because his clothes were wet from the rain during the night. He changed his clothes, put them in a side room, got a pan of water and washed, including his feet before putting on a different pair of shoes.

These shoes became key to his testimony and the evidence. The shoes he had worn during the search were high-top shoes (meaning above the ankle). The pair he put on that morning were considered low-top shoes. The clothes and shoes he wore before changing were submitted into evidence.

Permenter's testimony and cross-examination now turned to the handkerchief and statements attributed to him by others in previous testimony. His statement related to the handkerchief mirrored that of Nellie Permenter.

Swinton said that his brother, the now deceased Walter, had found the handkerchief while on a picnic with a large group at Indian Springs on the Fourth of July. Walter indicated that he found it on the ground near his buggy and had asked Swinton to find the owner. Swinton claimed to have put the handkerchief in his coat pocket and simply forgot about it. He had not worn the coat since that time and denied that it had been found in his pants pocket as some had previously stated. He also claimed that he knew nothing about the handkerchief as evidence against him until after his arrest.

His testimony then turned to statements attributed to him. He denied having any ill will toward the Sharp family. He denied making any remarks that could be construed as trying to misdirect the search and he denied any comments about a dog barking at a possum on the night of the search. His denials continued – never made the statement that the bloodhounds would track him because he had been in the woods near the location of the body and he repeated that he had never said that he had it in for "old man Sharp". In addition, he denied ever directly saying to Lee Sharp that it might have been a negro that killed Miss Janie. He said other men in the crowd were making suggestions as to who could have committed the crime and he did state that he didn't think there was anybody mean enough in the whole county to have killed her. He said that he heard several men say that when she was found, she would likely be bound and gagged and other similar statements.

When asked if he knew of any other young men that had courted Miss Janie. He specifically mentioned Earl Ray and Sol Whitmire. Interestingly, he could not remember if he had ever attended school with Janie.

When asked about the bloodhound, he said that the dog smelled around his father's property and went to the barn lot. Swinton claimed he was on the gallery and when the dog returned to the front of the home, he stepped off the porch and into the yard in an attempt to "test the brute". He said the dog went to a hole of water near the well where he was standing but that the dog never scented him.

Under cross-examination by Prosecutor Hill, Swinton was asked about his brother, Walter who had been killed just the week before. Little was said about this testimony but it was noted that Mrs. Permenter was deeply affected and broke down and wept.

Swinton was then asked about an accusation that had occurred early in the investigation. Hill asked if he had ever been indicted for assault or specifically for assaulting a little girl named Sistrunk. Permenter quickly denied both allegations but interestingly said that he had never been "convicted" in a justice or circuit court. There was no follow up to this question and no evidence was ever submitted related to these accusations.

While under cross-examination, he stated that – yes he had been in the company of several young women since receiving the handkerchief from his brother but never thought to find its owner.

Before leaving the stand, Permenter denied previous statements about Janie that were attributed to him. He denied saying to David Steed at a prayer meeting that he would give ten dollars and be willing to spend ten years in jail just to have illicit relations with Miss Janie. He also denied telling Bob McCool while at the home of Cyrus Ray that Janie was the prettiest girl he ever saw and if he couldn't have her – no one would.

A line of witnesses for the defense continued throughout the day. W.T. (or W. L.) Horn spoke about tracks that he had seen near an old stump. Out of curiosity, he and several others began their own investigation, searching for tracks and evidence. They started near Rural Hill and turned onto Commodore Road. Near a small ravine near where the body was discovered, they found evidence of a struggle and tracks of a woman and a man. There was one man's track near an old pine stump that was clear and well defined. He placed his foot in the track and it matched his shoe almost exactly – his size being an 81/2 or nine. A later comparison of his shoe with the one worn by Permenter that night was made during the trial. They did not match.

Swinton's parents were both called by the defense. Mrs. Permenter stated that as far as she knew her family and the Sharp family had been on friendly terms and she was not aware that Swinton had even had an interest in Miss Janie. She had left home on the day of the murder at around 2:00 pm. Swinton had already gone to the Hinze Post Office. She went by O.L. Permenter's home where O.L.'s wife joined her at the home of a neighbor, P. Shumaker where they spent the rest of the afternoon. It was here that she first learned about Miss Janie's disappearance from Earl and Forest Ray.

She returned home near sundown and found Swinton had just returned from the field where he was plowing. When they received the phone call about Miss Janie's disappearance, Swinton left there shortly thereafter without eating supper. He was wearing a blue serge coat and light tan high-top shoes. She did not see him again until the next morning when he came home to change clothes.

At this point, the defense recalled Martha Sharp, Janie's mother. When asked if she had spoken with Mrs. Permenter that evening, she acknowledged that she told Mrs. Permenter that Janie had gone to the store at Rural Hill to get cloth for a waist and she was told to hurry home. When she didn't return, Mrs. Sharp had sent her younger children to find her. This was not noted in her initial testimony.

When Janie's body was brought to the Sharp home, she said she could not look at her for a while but had found twenty-five cents of change in a pocket and it appeared that the pocket had been ripped or cut by the murderer.

Tom Gregory, Swinton's brother-in-law took the stand and testified that a week after the murder, he returned to the area and found tracks leading to the location where Janie's body was found. He believed that they were the tracks of a man and a woman.

Swinton's father, Ed Permenter was the next witness. He had not testified in the first trial. He corroborated Swinton's testimony stating that he had been plowing that afternoon, that they had changed horses and that he was sure Swinton had plowed until sundown. He admitted that during the evening of the search, several parties came to the house and inquired about Swinton. He also indicated that he and his family were cooperative and assisted the officers who came to get Swinton's clothes the next morning.

R. P. McAlilly was a justice of the peace in the area at the time and he testified to the state of Miss Janie's body, noting that there was very little blood at the scene.

McAlilly was the last witness of the day as court adjourned until the next morning.

16. REBUTTALS

THURSDAY, AUGUST 21, 1912

The defense was near the end of its witness list. In fact, the first witness called on Thursday morning was their last. Perninah Leech Ball was the grandmother of Janie Sharp. She was seventy-five years of age at the time of the trial. She indicated that Alma Ray, a family friend, had bought a dozen handkerchiefs for Mrs. Ball previously and Mrs. Ball had distributed them as gifts to her female grandchildren. Janie Sharp was one of those grandchildren. She admitted that she had not paid much attention to the handkerchiefs and could not remember what kind of border they had. Under cross-examination by the prosecution, she said that while at the Sharp home on the morning after the murder, she had been in the room with Janie's body and had not seen a handkerchief.

Prior to the rebuttal by the prosecution, the defense team submitted an additional piece of evidence – a letter from a chemist at the nearby Mississippi A & M College concerning the analysis of Swinton's clothing submitted into evidence. No traces of blood were found.

Swinton Permenter was then called to the stand by the prosecution for one additional question. Had he gone to the store at Rural Hill on the afternoon of the murder for some trimmings for his sister? He denied the act.

The prosecution began its rebuttal by focusing again on the handkerchief. Bessie Ray was called to the stand to identify the handkerchief submitted into evidence. She examined it and was definitive in her identification that it had indeed belonged to Jane. Defense counsel attempted to muddy the waters and question her certainty concerning the handkerchief but she never wavered in her testimony.

George Clark was the next witness. As a friend of the family, he made bond for Lon Burchfield who was originally arrested along with Permenter. Just prior to Burchfield's release, Clark was conversing with Burchfield and he told him that it was twenty minutes to two when they left the swimming hole on the day of the murder. This was in direct conflict with the timeline Burchfield testified to earlier in the trial. Clark indicated that he later visited Burchfield at his home and that they took walks and discussed the case prior to the first trial. In one case, Burchfield again stated that the time was twenty minutes to two and on another occasion as they were walking near the field he had been plowing on the day of the murder, Clark indicated that it was Burchfield who made the statement, "Do you reckon a man could do this amount of plowing from the time I went to the wash hole and get home at 3:30". This statement had been attributed to Swinton Permenter in earlier testimony.

Clark was asked about the veracity of a previous defense witness. The witness was identified at this juncture as Will Owens but this was most certainly the witness previously identified as Ed Owens. While Owens' testimony was not significant in the defense's case, the prosecution seemed to place importance on his poor character. Clark's testimony was that he did indeed know Owens and found him to be a man of poor character and that his reputation for speaking the truth was lacking.

Tom McCool, Hewlett Ray and Alonzo Hunt were called to speak of the character of Owens. Each had a similar opinion of Owens and Horn indicated that he knew that Owens had been convicted of assault in Oklahoma Indian Territory at the age of fifteen and had served time in a reformatory in Missouri. Horn told the court that he would not believe Owens under oath.

George Kelly, W.J. Webb and Benton Ray also took the stand and placed the defense's timeline into question. Kelly indicated that one of the Hobby boys told him that the young men left the swimming hole at 1:35 not 2:35. Webb corroborated this testimony. Benton Ray spoke of a conversation with Lon Burchfield who indicated that he left Swinton at 2:00 not 3:30 as Burchfield had previously testified. On the stand, Benton Ray indicated that he believed Swinton was guilty of the crime.

Swinton Permenter was recalled again by the prosecution and asked about a Sunday before the murder while at a gathering at the Cyrus Ray home. He was asked if Sol Whitney had actually been keeping time with Miss Janie on that evening and that in his jealousy didn't he say that she was the prettiest girl he ever saw and if he couldn't go with her then nobody else would. Permenter denied making such a statement.

Tom McCool in his testimony indicated that he heard Permenter make that statement.

Hardy Breazel, the father of the Breazel boys who had been at the swimming hole with Permenter was the next to testify and he contradicted his own son's testimony – stating that his son Ezra told him that the time so often stated by the defense was actually 1:40 pm not 2:25 or 2:35 pm.

J.F Shumacher, the owner of the other store in Rural Hill was called and testified that O.L. Permenter had been in his store around 3:45 pm on the afternoon of the murder and that Miss Janie had been there earlier in the day. His testimony was not significant.

The prosecution then presented two additional witnesses that brought the defense's time line into question. Grady Ray stated that she heard Swinton's sister, Nellie, state on the morning after the murder while at the Sharp home, that she had seen Swinton at the Tom Gregory place at around 3:00 pm. Another woman named Iva stated that she heard Nellie make the same statement.

In rebuttal, the defense did not address this statement but did call Reese Hobby, who was the father of the Hobby boys who were at the swimming hole with Swinton on the day of the murder. Hobby was called to rebut the testimony of Charlie Horn, a previous witness for the prosecution. Horn's testimony was not documented in the Commercial Appeal's articles but he apparently testified that he had been with the boys at the swimming hole. Hobby indicated that Horn did not go to the Hinze Post Office with his sons but did return with them after swimming.

Henry Ray was the last witness to testify in the trial. Henry married Effie Permenter, Swinton's cousin. He stated that on Christmas in 1911, seventeen months after the murder, he told his wife if she knew anything about Swinton's role in the murder that she had better tell it. She was offered $800 to tell what she knew (never stating from where that money would come) and that the family had received a letter stating that she knew all about the murder and she better tell it or she would get in trouble.

Both sides rested their case and the court was adjourned till 9:00 am on Friday morning. Closing arguments would be made and it was expected that the jury would receive the case sometime after noon. After one day of jury selection and nine days of testimony, the end of the long saga of Janie Sharp and Swinton Permenter was approaching.

17. CLOSING ARGUMENTS

FRIDAY & SATURDAY, AUGUST 22-23, 1912

If possible, the courtroom was even more crowded than before as press and interested parties wanted to be on hand for the conclusion of one of the most sensational trials in Mississippi history. Not all present were able to fit into the courtroom and the gallery was set aside for women only. The Montgomery County Sheriff brought in more deputies and stationed them about the room fearing that there might be outbursts upon the reading of the verdict. The Commercial Appeal noted that individuals from Starkville, Maben, Indianola and Gulfport were in the crowd.

On Swinton Permenter's side of the room were his parents, sisters Nellie and Eva and his married sisters, Mrs. Gregory and Mrs. Schumaker. Before the session opened, Swinton could be seen playing with one of his nieces at the railing. On the opposite side were Mr. and Mrs. Sharp, their daughter, Mrs. Morgan and their two remaining sons.

Court opened that morning with controversy. There was much legal haggling over the instructions to the jury. The details under contention were not disclosed but by 10:00 am, the matter had still not been settled and Judge McLean adjourned till 1:00 pm. Over the next few hours, the matter was settled and summations began promptly after lunch.

Judge McLean cautioned the crowd stating that he would not tolerate any outbursts or expressions of approval or disapproval in his courtroom.

The prosecution began their final argument with Hill as the first to speak. He simply reviewed the case and was considered effective. He was followed by R. B. Miller for the defense who spoke for nearly two hours, ridiculing the prosecution's case and making a plea for acquittal. J. B. Webb then spoke for the defense pointing out contradictions in the testimony of several of the state's witnesses and closed by stating that the physical facts of the case could point to nothing but acquittal of his client. He possibly suggested other scenarios under which the crime could have been committed including the possibility that Janie had been killed at Rural Hill and her body had been moved by wagon by a man and a woman. As darkness began to fall, former Judge J. H. Teat for the prosecution made a passionate case for conviction. His arguments were emotional and appeared to have a deep affect upon the Sharp family.

The case would not go to the jury just yet. There were still arguments to be made that would take a considerable amount of time. At 7:00 pm, Judge McLean told a disappointed courtroom that arguments would resume on Saturday.

******

The next morning, the courtroom was again packed as closing

arguments were to continue. As the court convened, Defense Attorney Miller made a motion to close the arguments. His reasoning was that the state had opened and closed the summations on the previous day and both sides had had their opportunities to make their case. Judge McLean was not moved however and he instructed further statements to continue.

Speaking for the defense was W.F. Thompson. Thompson's approach was to castigate the Sharp family and their supporters for their hasty and determined conviction that Swinton Permenter had committed the crime. Their rush to judgment had blinded them to any other possibilities – the real possibility that someone other than Permenter had taken Miss Janie's life on that July day more than two years ago. He appealed to the jury to not allow blind prejudice and passion over the brutal crime to lead to the conviction of an innocent man.

The final statement for the defense was made by H.H. Rogers, one of Swinton's attorneys from the first trial. He reviewed Permenter's alibi in great detail and proceeded to attack any prosecution witnesses that cast doubt upon the timeline. He was especially harsh when it came to Hardy Breazel who contradicted his own son's testimony about the time that the youths left the swimming hole.

Rogers also pointed out that the shoe evidence, initially presented by the prosecution, did not support their case. He noted the testimony by C.B. Ray that indicated that the supposed track of the killer did not match the shoes won by Permenter on the day of the murder.

As it was nearly the noon hour, Judge McLean recessed until 1:00 pm when the prosecution would have its last opportunity to present its argument.

That afternoon, District Attorney Thomas Lamb made the final statement for the prosecution. His approach was to lay out the state's theory of the murder for the jury. The state contended that Swinton Permenter had not returned to the field to plow that afternoon. That upon returning from the swimming hole at an earlier time than defense witnesses stated, his sister Nellie Permenter had sent him to Rural Hill to purchase some dress goods from one of the stores. Along the route, he met Miss Janie in a lonely spot, forced her into the woods and subsequently killed her in a brutal manner.

He recapped the testimony of numerous witnesses concerning his strange behavior during the search and he also covered the statements attributed to him by others in testimony concerning his desire and interest in Janie. He then cast doubt upon the testimony of Swinton's family members noting that it would be expected of them to defend him even if it meant lying under oath.

He came to the defense of Hardy Breazel, who had the unenviable task of contradicting his own son on the stand. Lamb indicated that the state believed that the younger Breazel had been threatened with charges of perjury if he didn't support the time line presented by other defense witnesses.

Lamb then attacked the defense's alternate theory of the crime. Defense Attorney Miller had suggested that Janie had actually been killed at Rural Hill, her body placed in a sack and carried to the wooded branch by a man and a woman where the body was found. There is no indication as to who these people might have been and was likely one of many rumors that had developed in the community after the crime. Lamb ridiculed the story and said there was no evidence to support it.

Lamb closed his argument with an appeal for the jury to fulfill their responsibility and insure that justice was done in this case.

His final statements were to review the graphic and brutal manner in which Miss Janie Sharp had been murdered.

The emotional arguments were now completed. The Sharp family had endured the process but had wept openly at times. According to newspaper reports, Swinton Permenter seemed calm and showed little emotion during the final statements – just as he had done throughout the trial.

With the final statements made at 3:30 pm, the jury was provided with instruction by Judge McLean and retired to deliberate at 3:55 pm. Permenter remained in the courtroom and was seen smoking a pipe and cigarettes throughout the evening as he waited to learn his fate.

Deliberations continued for four hours without reaching a verdict. At 8:00 pm, the jurors retired for the evening. The trial of Swinton Permenter would continue for at least one more day.

18. VERDICT

SUNDAY, AUGUST 24, 1912

This two-year drama began on a county road near Rural Hill, Mississippi in 1910 with the brutal murder of an attractive young woman ready to start her adult life. It was about to culminate in a packed, sweltering courtroom in the small town of Winona, Mississippi; a courtroom where the fate of another young person was to be decided – freedom or death at the end of a noose. Through these two years, a whole county was divided. Feelings ran high and even families were torn between their support of the victim's family and the belief in the innocence of a young man named Swinton Permenter.

From almost the beginning, the Sharp family never wavered in their belief in Swinton's guilt. The Permenter family likewise rallied to their youngest son, resolute in their certainty of his innocence. These two years also saw the blatant murders of two men; murders that were almost certainly tied to the case- and murders in which no one was ever brought to justice.

Both sides had presented their cases, evidence was produced, rebuttals made and lengthy summations presented. It was now all in the hands of a jury of twelve men.

A Sunday court session was a rarity but given the length of the trial and with nothing left to do but wait for the jury to make its decision, Judge McLean stood ready to resume if a verdict was reached. It didn't take long.

The jurors began their deliberation early that morning and by 8:50 am, the twelve men of Montgomery County filed back into the jury box. Swinton Permenter stood to hear his fate as his family and the Sharp family looked on in anticipation.

Judge McLean asked, "Gentlemen, have you agreed upon a verdict?'

C.L. Moore, the selected foreman of the jury stated, "Yes, sir, we have."

The slip of paper holding the decision was passed to the Court Clerk named Ford. There was dead silence in the crowded courtroom as all waited for the verdict.

In a deliberate tone, Clerk Ford read,

"We the jury, find the defendant not guilty."

There was no outburst in the courtroom as was feared, no gasp of despair or relief, only a low, almost inaudible murmur. Swinton Permenter seemed stunned, the Sharp family was devastated.

Before dismissing the court, Judge McLean spoke to the jury. He thanked them for their service and stated that the case had been moved to Winona because the court was familiar with the nature of juries in the community and knew that their actions would be just and right. While he served and respected the people of the whole judicial district, he brought the case to his hometown for those reasons. He again thanked them for their patient consideration of the evidence and the arguments presented by the attorneys and that he believed that the verdict was one based on a fair and impartial consideration of the evidence presented and the law. Their verdict could not be criticized.

The jury foreman C. L, Moore responded and thanked the court and the Montgomery County Sheriff for the many kindnesses extended to them during their confinement and deliberation.

The jury was released and the court dismissed. The Permenter family was elated. While Swinton still sat as if numb, his father, mother and sisters rose and went forward to shake the hands of each juror. Ed Permenter was heard to say, "Thank God, my poor boy is free! He never killed that girl!"

Mrs. Permenter was overcome with emotion as tears flowed down her face. She grabbed her son, kissed him and held him in a long embrace.

In an action that would seem odd or even inappropriate by today's standards, the jury returned to the jury room and were soon joined by the Permenter family. Swinton addressed the jurors – thanking them for their decision.

*****

The Sharp family was broken, distraught and angry. While speaking with reporters, Will Sharp bitterly repeated his conviction of Permenter's guilt. "...a crying shame that such a result could have been reached. If they were to bring another man charged with this crime, I'd say nobody but Swinton Permenter murdered her!"

Lee Sharp, Janie's older brother, was livid. He had been convinced of Swinton's guilt from the beginning and taken an active role in the affair. *"He is a scoundrel and it is dangerous to turn loose in any community such a heartless brute!"*

After more than two years of suspicion, months of imprisonment in Louisville, Winona and a Hinds County jail, a conviction and death sentence and the loss of his brother, Swinton Permenter was now a free man. Regardless, his life would be changed forever.

Due to the emotion of the Sharp family and friends, Swinton was guarded by a county deputy throughout that day until he left Winona that evening. His destination was closely guarded; all that was disclosed – "headed to some point not known. "

The Sharp's and Permenter's returned to their homes in Rural Hill that evening by train. Some evidence suggests that both families took the same train. Reports at the community of Durant indicated that both families were subjected to curious onlookers, the Sharps receiving sympathy, the Permenters, the object of inquisitive stares. Upon disembarking, the Sharps were met at the McCool depot by a large crowd who expressed their sympathy due to the outcome of the case. Lee Sharp told many in the crowd, *"They turned a guilty man loose."*

One of the most sensational trials in Mississippi history was over yet there was no resolution to Janie Sharp's murder; no justice, no punishment, no sense of closure for her family or for the communities of Rural Hill, Louisville and Winston County. The trial may have been over, but the story was not.

WINSTON COUNTY JOURNAL

AUGUST 30, 1912

BLOODY CLOTHES FOUND

Mister George Hinze, who was the returning officer of the election held Wednesday from Rural Hill brought the news that a bundle of rotten clothing consisting of a pair of drawers, socks and what is supposed to be an undershirt was found by Gus Burns about a quarter mile from where Miss Janie Sharp was found murdered July 22, 1910.

The clothing was found partially under an old rotten log. The clothes were in a paper sack and so decayed that it was difficult to tell just what garments they are and they are of course supposed to have blood on them. Doctor W.W. Clement, dentist of the Rural Hill community was in town Thursday and was asked by your writer what he thought of the find. Doctor Clement does not think it has any connection with the young lady's death and treats the matter with little concern. The finder of this bundle of clothing has not yet brought them in to the officers.

After that article, no further mention of these garments were made. It is not known if they ever existed and possibly the story was fabricated as it surfaced immediately after the trial. If the bag of clothing was ever submitted to the Winston County Sheriff, no record exists of further investigation.

KOSCIUSKO COURIER

SEPTEMBER 6, 1912

SOME PRETTY SHARP CRITICISM

The verdict of the jury in the Permenter case is a disgrace to Mississippi manhood. The law that requires a jury where an indictment is for murder to bring in a verdict of guilty as charged, or clear, is a travesty of justice and the courts of Mississippi are a farce.

If it's a case of blind tiger whiskey, or negro crap game, shooting on public highway, carrying concealed weapons where the jury can get the fee and justice the costs, there is no possible doubt of conviction. But let the villain have money to hire lawyers, with the law so fixed that a man who has any sense or can read a paper, or is even qualified to form an opinion, he is disqualified to sit on the jury. None but the most ignorant are jurors and they are made to believe that if there is a shadow of a doubt they shall acquit, and nine tenths of them don't really know what would be a doubt.

Now jurors should be allowed to bring in a verdict of guilty for less than murder in the first degree in such cases, and give verdict for imprisonment for 15 to 15 years.

Now from this Permenter verdict Miss Janie Sharp was not killed or out-raged at all, the whole thing being a nightmare and the jury believes she is still going to the Hinze post office after the mail. That is about all the reasonable doubt the jury could have had, judging from the evidence published in the Commercial Appeal. Now is it any wonder that lynch law is in evidence?

I always try to obey the law, but should a daughter of mine be treated in such a manner, I would kill the villain and any officer who tried to keep me from it, and would join any mob to rid the country of such brutes in this kind of case. If we are to hound the poor devil that sells whiskey or carries a pistol, or the negro who shoots craps to the extreme as is done, and turn rapists and murderers loose on the people, better stop the farce of courts as they now are and let each man protect his own home.

It is almost impossible to convict a scoundrel in Mississippi but an honest and truthful man can't get justice at all for the scoundrel will lie and you are told this makes the "reasonable doubt."

Jehosaphat! how we need some old fashioned justice meted out from our courts.

The people are holding the laws in contempt and justly so.

Now I suggest to stop all courts until the law can be made adequate for such cases.

Dr. R. J. Heald, M.D.

19. SPECULATION

Whether the public agreed with the verdict or not, observers would agree that the legal system of Mississippi worked as it should in the case of Swinton Permenter. An initial rush to judgment and conviction were overturned on solid grounds and ultimately a well-structured and ordered trial took place that allowed a jury to weigh all the evidence before passing judgment.

In truth, almost all of the evidence was circumstantial and there was direct conflict of testimony of a multitude of witnesses. An impartial jury had no real option but to find Swinton Permenter not guilty based upon the evidence. But does that mean that he didn't commit the crime of murder?

The investigation of the crime left much to be desired. Swinton was arrested and charged quickly and with resources focused on his guilt, there was no investigation into other possibilities. There was little focus on hard evidence or attempts to exclude others as suspects. In reality, the investigation of this case was probably beyond the capabilities of law enforcement. This is not a condemnation of the Winston County Sheriff but simply a reality of the times.

Sheriffs in Mississippi were elected officials and still are to this day. While things have changed considerably and law enforcement has become more professional, at that time no qualifications were required except to be electable. Most law enforcement involved breaking up fights, settling disputes between neighbors and rousing the occasional drunkard. There were no real investigative skills, little need for them and certainly no source to obtain them. The concepts of modern day forensics and chains of evidence were not to be pursued until the latter half of the twentieth century. Given the lack of a direct eyewitness, possession of a murder weapon or an admission of guilt, the local law probably did the best that they could.

In examining the evidence against Permenter, there are several points that can't be overlooked:

The murder weapon(s) – It was believed that Janie was struck in the head by a blunt heavy object. Some speculated that it may have been the butt of a pistol. Permenter was seen in the possession of a pistol on the night of the murder but little was made of it. All indications are that it was not examined for blood evidence and no attempt was made to compare it to the wound on Janie's head. Based upon the limited trial records, it was not submitted into evidence.

Janie was stabbed multiple times in an apparent attempt to assure her death. A Barlow knife, a relatively small folding pocket knife was found in Permenter's clothes. Again it was apparently not examined in detail as it was only casually submitted as evidence as an item in his possession along with the handkerchief. There was nothing to indicate that a search for another knife was ever undertaken.

Blood evidence – The general consensus was that Janie struggled with her attacker and possibly escaped his grasp while he was in pursuit. This, in addition to the brutal nature of the crime, would lead one to believe that there would in fact be blood on the murderer's clothing and person. The location of the body indicated very little blood was present which may have suggested that Janie was killed elsewhere and the body placed here after her death. If this was a crime of opportunity as the prosecution suggested, it is likely that Permenter would have also had blood transfer to his clothing in the process of moving Janie's body. After chemical analysis, no blood evidence was found on his garments.

Lack of wounds – All evidence indicated that Janie fought her attacker as he pursued her. Knowing that she was fighting for her life and that she was a strong healthy young woman, it would be reasonable to assume that she may have scratched, clawed or bruised the killer. There was no mention of wounds upon Permenter or that he was even examined closely for such wounds.

The body and the crime scene – Janie's body and the crime scene were likely not examined properly. Given the emotion at the time this could be expected. Given the despair of the family, the sensibilities of the time, the condition of the body and the heat of a July summer, Janie was buried quickly leaving some questions forever unanswered.

The crime scene was likely a mess. With a crowd of searchers and later curious "investigators", any evidence would have been trampled or contaminated. Tracks attributed to the killer could have just as easily been those of any in the crowd.

Opportunity – The swimming hole on Lobutcha Creek was three and one half miles from Rural Hill and likely two to two and a half from the crime scene - no short distance on foot or even by horseback. The Permenter home was four miles from Rural Hill as stated in the trial. Under the defense scenario, it would have been nearly impossible for Swinton to have returned to the Hinze post office and then after leaving the Burchfields make his way to the

Commodore Road near Rural Hill and commit the crime at the
time estimated. It would then also indicate that his sisters and
father had lied on his behalf under oath.

If the defense's timeline was incorrect, it would require that the
Burchfield boys, and the Hobbys were either all mistaken about the
time or they were all lying for Swinton. And again, it would
require his sisters and father to participate in the lie.

Motive – Much was made of previous comments by Swinton
concerning Janie, comments that seemed inappropriate in
hindsight. Unfortunately, such comments are commonly made by
young men about young women and are not necessarily grounds
for murder.

Was there more to the relationship between Swinton and Janie
Sharp than was exposed in the trials? Probably. Will Sharp's
almost immediate suspicion that Janie may have eloped with
someone other than her proclaimed fiancée, Earl Ray and his
request for Doctor Clemmons to search for Permenter on the
afternoon of the murder suggests that he suspected some sort of
relationship between the two young people. The immediate
suspicion cast upon Swinton, particularly by Janie's brother, Lee,
also indicated that he believed that there was more to the
relationship.

Speculation on this relationship has run rampant over the years and
some have suggested that Janie's engagement to Earl Ray was a
ruse perpetrated to hide her love affair with Swinton from a
disapproving father.

The handkerchief was the strongest evidence presented by the
prosecution in both trials. It was the one bit of physical evidence
that could tie Swinton to the crime. But there were problems here
that the jury could not likely overlook. Swinton had a plausible

explanation for its possession that was supported by his sister's testimony – a found item, forgotten and tucked into a coat pocket. When taken with the uncertainty of whether the handkerchief was found in Swinton's coat pocket or his pants pocket and that one witness testified that she saw a handkerchief near the body as it lay in the Sharp home, the evidence was not conclusive.

The bloodhound's identification yields some interesting possibilities but again, after thought, any conclusion becomes clouded. Did Ruth Hindoo scent Swinton that morning in the yard of the Permenter home as his trainer and several witnesses testified or was the dog's behavior more indecisive than stated? Were the hound's actions influenced by his trainer and the crowd?

The other possibility remains that because Swinton had been in those woods earlier, the dog tracked him rather than the real killer.

Much was made of Swinton's behavior on the night of the search. Several, including Lee Sharp testified that Swinton at times acted disinterested, evasive and made misleading statements in a possible attempt to lead the searchers away from the body. On the stand, Permenter denied making these statements. He either lied to protect himself or a number of others lied in an attempt to wrongfully incriminate him. This certainly presented a dilemma for the jury.

In spite of all these issues, there are some circumstances under which Swinton could have committed the crime. Three possibilities seem to stand out:

If the prosecution's timeline was correct and Swinton returned home a full forty-five minutes earlier that the defense presented and if his family was lying to cover his involvement, there would be sufficient time for him to have traveled the distance, especially on horseback. If he had traveled to Rural Hill on an errand for his sister, it is very likely that he could have encountered Janie on Commodore Road and committed the bloody act. However, this would have required the Burchfields and the Hobby's to provide misleading testimony concerning the time.

This raises another possibility that someone else who had been at that swimming hole could have participated in the murder, helped Swinton cover his tracks and concocted a different timeline to hide their involvement.

The third possibility is intriguing but less likely. If Swinton and Janie were lovers, had they arranged a clandestine meeting on that afternoon? Had Janie rejected his advances or had she informed him of her plans to marry Earl Ray. Had this rejection led to a fit of rage leading to Swinton making good on the statement attributed to him - "If he couldn't go with her, nobody else would?"

The fact that there was little effort to investigate any other possibilities concerning the murder is disturbing. It does seem unlikely that an outsider could have committed the crime. No one saw any strangers in the area and they would have been noticed in such a small and close knit community.

Although unverifiable today, a story surfaced at some point after the trial, that a letter written on stationary from the Peabody Hotel in Memphis had been received at the Winston County Courthouse. The anonymous author of this letter supposedly confessed to the crime stating that he had been passing through the area at the time. The accuracy of this report cannot be verified and there is no remaining evidence of such a letter.

There were certainly others from the community who could have committed the act. It was a rural area and it could certainly be a crime of opportunity – a young woman walking alone would seem an easy target for some.

Swinton had made the statement in prison that he believed he knew who committed the crime and that they had testified against him (at least in the first trial) His implication was that there were two men involved although it was never stated publicly who he believed they were.

Thomas McElroy and Hewlett Ray were the most likely candidates due to their "arrest" by Ben Walker. But no evidence was ever presented to show their involvement and the complete and utter dismissal of any evidence by the prosecution would suggest that they had no involvement.

In closing arguments, the possibility that Janie had actually been killed while in Rural Hill and that a man and woman had been involved (almost certainly local folk) seems farfetched as well. No evidence was ever provided to support this theory or to identify the parties involved.

It is interesting to note that no suspicion was cast upon any blacks in the community. It is certain in that day and time that if there had been any evidence in that direction, it would have been investigated further. Nothing in statements or trial testimony cast any suspicions in that direction.

Over the years, various theories have been put forward concerning who actually killed Miss Janie Sharp and almost all without substance. I won't address them here and besmirch the names of these individuals here due to the lack of any real evidence.

In the 1980's and 1990's, a local man named Louis Taunton sparked interest in the case again. Taunton was an amateur genealogist who had written, co-written and compiled a number of books on Winston County history as well as a weekly newspaper column. It was believed that he was in the process of writing a book about the Janie Sharp case and had intimated to a number of individuals that he had sufficient evidence to name the killer. There were rumors of a deathbed confession. The book never seemed to materialize and Taunton passed away in the early 2000's.

It has been reported that Taunton's wife had planned to donate his papers (including any related to this case) to the Winston County Library but Mrs. Taunton has since passed away as well and most of his papers never materialized. Some have reported that the hard drive of the computer believed to hold the book draft was found to be erased clean - just another mystery in the case of Janie Sharp.

One of the few remaining photographs of
Perninah Jane Sharp

Only known image of
Swinton Permenter

The Sharp family – possibly taken on July 23, 1910 – the
day of Janie's funeral. Bottom row: Will Sharp-Janie's father 2nd from
left, Martha-Janie's mother 4th from left,
Lee Sharp on right

l. to R sitting: Sheriff A.P. Hull, James Ming, Calvin Palmer, J.A. Hatcher, M.H. Hannah, J.O. Landrum, H.O. Houston, l. to R standing Bailiffs: W.H. Lovorn & C.A. Jones, Prentiss Adcock, A.L. Jackson, Ike Yarbrough, Frank Hindman, J.W. Edwards, D.C. Coleman, Bailiffs: W.E. Murphy & J.W. Triplett

Photo of 1st jury in Winston County

Postcard of Main Street Louisville in 1909 – Courthouse can be seen in center of photograph

All that remains of Montgomery County Courthouse in Winona – monument to Confederate soldiers & marker stone

20. AFTERMATH

Janie Sharp had been murdered while walking home along a wooded country lane on a hot July afternoon in 1910 near the backwoods community of Rural Hill, Mississippi. Suspicions fell immediately upon a young man, Swinton Permenter, not yet eighteen himself. A two-year ordeal ensued that included a trial and conviction, a Supreme Court ruling that overturned the conviction, suspicions cast upon others, the murders of two men and a second trial that was a sensation across Mississippi and the South.

When the Mississippi dust settled, no one was brought to justice for Janie's murder or those of Ben Walker, an investigator of the crime, and Walter Permenter, the brother of the suspect. To this day, no one can say who committed these crimes and anyone who may have had firsthand knowledge of the events of the day are long gone.

The Sharp's were convinced of Swinton's guilt and apparently made no further attempts to find any other suspects. There is no evidence that local law enforcement made any further investigation. Either it was believed that Swinton Permenter got away with the murder of Janie Sharp or there was simply no further evidence to pursue.

The lack of closure in the case fueled debate, hard feelings and suspicion not only in Rural Hill but in much of Winston County. Almost everyone was a relation or a friend to one or both families. Speculations and accusations continued for many years after the crime and in some forms still exist today.

Up until the 1970's, students in local schools were forbidden to write about the murder for fear of opening old wounds. I was recently contacted by one individual who stated that the only thing he had ever seen his grandparents argue over was the guilt or innocence of Swinton Permenter. Emotions ran high for many years and rumors of death threats surfaced often when someone began asking too many questions.

As a result, speculation turned to rumor, rumor intermingled with truth and the story became more sensational over the years. Soon, Janie became the subject of legend; a ghost story to tell and embellish as the years went by. It seemed that each year the story became more gruesome, bloody and fantastic - and visiting Janie's grave is now a favorite rite of passage for local high school kids on Halloween night; kids who know nothing about the real events of Janie's death and the drama that followed.

The people of Rural Hill and Winston County went back to their farms and businesses and continued their lives. The November presidential election provided some diversion from the case.

While campaigning in October, 1912, Teddy Roosevelt was the victim of an assassination attempt when a deranged man shot him in the chest with a 32 caliber revolver. The bullet was diverted and slowed by a glasses case and the manuscript of the speech that Roosevelt was about to give. The bullet was lodged near his heart but heroically, Roosevelt gave his campaign speech before seeking medical attention. In spite of the positive publicity, Woodrow Wilson won the election easily.

Locally the community was abuzz a few months later when two prisoners who were incarcerated on drunk and disorderly charges attempted to burn down the Winston County jail and courthouse.

Damage was limited but prophetically, the fire did spark calls for a citywide water system.

The case of Janie Sharp and Swinton Permenter continued to surface and create speculation especially due to other fire related events that may have had no connection with the case at all.

In January 1913, the home of W. J. Tabor on East Main Street in Louisville burned to the ground. Tabor was the employer of Walter Permenter and was rumored to have provided significant financial resources toward Swinton's defense. The fire was almost surely accidental based upon investigation but that didn't stop speculation as to the cause and a possible connection to the case.

Rumors and accusations boiled over in April of 1913 when a major fire swept through downtown Louisville. A large section of the northern block of Main Street was destroyed. It was believed the early morning fire started in a livery stable on the north side of the block and swept through some warehouse structures before destroying the Post Office, a bank, some offices and several stores that included the drug store belonging to W.J. Tabor. His connection to the case prompted accusations of arson by those on both sides.

The cause of the fire was never fully determined and there is no evidence that the fire was connected to the actions of anyone involved in the Janie Sharp affair.

Gradually the situation calmed and folks returned to their everyday lives. Louisville continued to grow and became a center of the timber and heavy equipment industry – a quiet, peaceful little community in central Mississippi. But what happened to the principal characters in this story?

Cyrus Ray (Janie's Uncle) and his family stayed in the Rural Hill area until his death in 1939. While many of his family are buried in the Rural Hill Cemetery, Cyrus and his wife are interred at the Hinze Baptist Church Cemetery located south of Rural Hill.

Doctor William M. Clement and his family eventually left the Rural Hill community and moved his practice to Louisville. He died in 1939 and is buried in the Masonic Cemetery.

While Forrest Ray did not appear to play a major role in the Janie Sharp case, his tragic death on Christmas Day in 1920 did stir interest. Sometime after the trial, he moved his family to the Beaumont- Port Arthur, Texas area where he served as a policeman in the community of Sour Lake. In the early morning hours of Saturday, Christmas Day, Ray was on duty and sitting in the unfinished vestibule of a new office building under construction. A young man approached on the street and fired five shotgun blasts through a plate glass window striking Ray several times. Ray initially survived the attack but passed a few hours later. A young oilfield worker named Sidney Oliver was taken into custody and eventually tried and convicted of the crime. Strangely enough, after multiple trials, Oliver only served one year in prison for the act.

Walter Edward Permenter was killed by a shotgun blast in 1912 in Eupora. His murder was never solved. No record of his murder or its investigation can be found in county records. The only references to his death can be found in newspaper reports. He is buried at the Masonic Cemetery in the center of Louisville, Ms. He left a widow (Madie A. Burch Permenter) and three children. She soon left Rural Hill and moved to Kemper county to live with her parents. She then moved to Philadelphia, Ms. where she served as a mail clerk with the Post Office. She never remarried. She died in 1969 and is buried next to her husband in Louisville along with two of their children.

Hulett or Hewlett Ray, one of the two men accused by Ben Walker of the crime moved to Oklahoma not long after the second trial and where he registered for the draft during WWI. He and his wife raised five children and he lived to a ripe old age in Oklahoma and is buried there.

Thomas McElroy (also accused by Ben Walker) was married to a sister of Hewlett and Earl Ray. Little is known about his whereabouts after the trial and most assumed he returned to Texas but it seems likely that he stayed in the area or returned at some point. He and his wife are buried at Doty Springs Cemetery in Attala County not far from Rural Hill. He passed away in 1946 at the age of seventy-three.

Ben Walker was killed in 1912 in the home of Elbert Vowell in Winston County. His killer was never captured or identified. There is no record of further investigation into his death beyond the night he died. Nothing is known about his past and his body was never claimed by family members. He is buried in the Smallwood or Wood Cemetery located a few miles south and west of Rural Hill.

Earl Ray, the "fiancée" of Janie Sharp, married in 1914 and continued to live in Mississippi and the general area. He raised several children and passed away in Choctaw County in the 1960's.

Elbert Vowell is believed to have remained in the general area but is sometimes referenced as James Elbert Vowell. There is some evidence that he moved to Leake County, Mississippi by 1930.

Judge George A. McLean's term as Circuit Court Judge expired in September, 1912. The conduct of the final trial of Swinton Permenter was a sort of triumph for him after the earlier conviction was overturned. Almost immediately after the trial, he was honored by the local bar for his service on the court.

The Will Sharp family stayed in Rural Hill for a short while after the trial, but in 1913, they sold their property and most of the immediate family packed their belongings and moved to Bryan, Oklahoma. Much of the family still live in that area today. Janie's Father, Will, passed away in 1919 at the age of sixty-one. Martha Sharp suffered a stroke not long after the trial and lived her remaining years as an invalid. She passed just one year after her husband in 1920. They are buried in Calera, Oklahoma. Lee Sharp lived until the age of sixty-nine and is buried in Texas.

At the time of the move, the Rural Hill property including the house was sold to Jesse Barfield. The home burned to the ground in 1921.

The Permenter family apparently stayed in Mississippi although at some point, they sold their property in Rural Hill. Records show that Swinton's parents, Edward and Anna are buried in the Hopewell Baptist Cemetery in Choctaw County, Mississippi. Edward died in 1932 and Anna passed away in 1942. Swinton's siblings remained in Mississippi as well and at least one stayed in the immediate area.

Swinton Permenter's whereabouts immediately after the trial are not known. It is doubtful, that he ever returned to the Rural Hill area for any length of time. Much of the following information here is not certain but was accumulated from various sources. It is believed that he lived for a period of time in Okolona, Mississippi, possibly in the home of his sister. He entered military service during WWI. Some have indicated that he initially enlisted under the false name, Jesse Jackson. If so, this was corrected as later military records indicate his real name. These records indicate that he was born in 1895. The was most certainly incorrect as he was seventeen at the time of the murder.

There is also some evidence that he lived and worked in the oil fields in Texas and Oklahoma for a period of time but he is listed in the 1930 census as a resident of Bolivar, County, Ms. and residing in the household of his younger sister.

At some time after 1930, he apparently married a woman named Bernice from Avery County, North Carolina and it is likely that he lived in that area for a period of time. There is little information about the marriage and no indication of children.

In his later years, Swinton apparently suffered from health problems and may have suffered paralysis in his legs and possibly his hands. As a result, he spent the last years of his life in a Veterans' Administration home in Johnson City, Tennessee, as this was listed as his last address.

Swinton Permenter died on August 16, 1946 and is buried at the Mountain Home National Cemetery in Johnson City, Tennessee. There is no indication that he spoke of the trial in later life and it is likely that those around him knew nothing about the murder of which he was accused.

Janie Sharp lost her life on July 21, 1910. She is buried not at Rural Hill but in the Center Ridge Methodist Church Cemetery located several miles east of Rural Hill. This cemetery was probably chosen because her sister, an infant was previously buried here.

*****

Janie Sharp's murder was never solved. It has now been more than one hundred years since her brutalized body was found just off Commodore Road in the Rural Hill Community. It has almost been that long since the unsolved murders of Ben Walker and Walter Permenter. Over that time the area has changed significantly.

Rural Hill was never more than a small village but it was full of life. Two stores, a post office, a church, a two room school and even a small mill that produced wooden spokes were the center of a small group of farms and the families that worked them. There was no railroad and no county courthouse and it was inevitable that Rural Hill would slowly decline like hundreds of other communities across Mississippi and the South. Over the years, the Post Office closed and mail delivery moved to McCool. The schools in the area were consolidated and closed. Automobiles became more affordable and travel became quicker and easier and the need for the stores diminished as well.

Today, there is no evidence of any structures except for the Church. Rural Hill United Methodist Church suffers from declining membership and no longer holds regular services but it continues to survive and is well maintained. Memorial in May always draws a crowd of people whose ancestors founded the Church or grew up within its shadow.

The Commodore Road along which Janie's body was found, was never much more than a trail. Its location is now on private property and is no longer maintained. The Neal Ray Road where the Sharp home and the Permenter home were located does still exist and although it is a very narrow, gravel thoroughfare, it is well maintained by the county. The homesteads are long gone but one can identify locations that might indicate an old home site. There are still a few folks who can specifically identify the location where Janie's body was found. I was contacted by an individual who provided helpful information that indicated that some evidence of Janie's moss covered tracks (heel prints) may have existed into the 1960's although I find this very unlikely.

Janie Sharp's grave is located in the Center Ridge United Methodist Church Cemetery. It is the tallest monument in the cemetery and located near the road. A sister who died as an infant is buried beside her.

Her epitaph reads as follows:

"Sleep On, Dear Janie, Thy Work is Done

Thy Mortal Pangs are O'er

Jesus Has Come And Borne Thee Home

Beyond This World Of Sin And Woe"

At one time, the monument was vandalized and the top marble ornament was stolen but later found along a roadside. Since that time, gracious church members provided the means to restore the monument and attach the top ornament permanently. It has become a favorite place for teenagers to gather at Halloween and the area is the subject of many ghost stories that of course, involve Janie and her murder.

There are a great deal of details and mostly hearsay about this event that were not directly included in this narrative; some because they were merely rumor, others because they may not have been pertinent as told.

One interesting bit of information not previously included was a Winston County Journal article that indicated that a set of bloody clothes were found hidden under a fallen log, almost immediately after the final trial. It stated that the garments showed much decay and were to be brought to the sheriff's office for examination.

After that article, no further mention of these garments was ever made. It is not known by this writer if they ever existed, were never submitted to the sheriff, or were determined to not be pertinent to the case. In any event, they were never mentioned again.

The murder of Miss Janie Sharp remains a mystery. Her death was brutal and tragic and touched the lives of many in the community. One individual was moved to write a poem about her that was published in the Winston County Journal only days after her death and it has survived over the years. Some evidence exists that the poem was even set to music and has been referred to as "The Ballad of Janie Sharp":

In Memory of Miss Janie Sharp

An April birth
Upon this earth
To live mid sin and strife
Though bright and gay
Hath been her stay
A short but happy life

Two years ago
As some may know
E'ver sweet sixteen was o'er
She said one day
"I've left sin's way
To walk therein no more"

Just eighteen years
Of toil and tears
Hath crowned her life with joy
A friend was made
While here she staid
With most each girl and boy

One pleasant day
While on the way
Back to her home so sweet,
By criminal beast
Her journey ceased for straggling death to meet

Her life was pure
It would not endure
One thought of virtues flight
She doubtless sighed
And then replied:
"It will all be brought to light"

That heartless whelp
Stopped cries for help
For fear they might be heard
No doubt his cry
Was "you shall die
To never tell a word"

And there alone
While friends are gone
The helpless girl was slain
She could not tell
Her friend "farewell"
Nor see her home again

Through pains untold
Did gates unfold
The angels called her home
"Come Janie dear,
And live up here
Where you'll be safe to roam"

A noble one
That priceless one
Whose friends are sad with grief
Hath fled away
To endless day

And there hath found relief

Her path as bright
Was filled with light
For many friends she made
Her life was sweet
With smiles to greet
While she with pleasure staid

That voice so clear
No more we hear
To pledge her friendship true
For she hath gone
To heaven's throne
And waits to welcome you

Her pains are o'er
She sighs no more
Nor pressed with earthly care
With crown so bright
And clothed in white
She sings with angels there

      T. F. Horn
      Hinze, Ms.

SOURCES

- THE TRIAL for the MURDER of PERNINAH JANIE SHARP by Lucille Wood
- TRIAL OF SWINTON PERMENTER FOR THE MURDER OF MISS JANIE SHARP JULY 21,1910 by Ruby C. Hurt.
- Winston County Journal – Louisville, Ms.
- The Commercial Appeal – Memphis, Tn.
- The Jackson Daily News – Jackson, Ms.
- Winston County Circuit Clerk
- Winston County Library – Louisville, Ms.
- Attala County Library – Kosciusko, Ms.
- Tupelo Man – the Life and Times of George McLean, a Most Peculiar Newspaper Publisher by Robert Blade
- http://www.genealogy.com
- http://www.msrailroads.com
- http://msgw.org
- Star Herald – Kosciusko, Ms.
- Star-Ledger – Kosciusko, Ms.
- Kosciusko Star – Kosciusko, Ms.
- Kosciusko Courier – Kosciusko, Ms.
- A History of Winston County, Volume 2, by Jennie Newsom Hoffman
- The Progress Warden – Eupora, Ms.
- Beaumont Enterprise – Beaumont, Tx.
- The Palestine Journal – Palestine, Texas
- http://www.findagrave.com
- http://www.ancestry.com
- Interview with Harry Bernard Tabor – Winston County, Ms.
- Winston County, Ms. Sheriff Jason Pugh
- http://winston.msgen.info

The tragic tale of Janie Sharp has remained a topic of discussion in the area for more than one hundred years. Speculation, hearsay and the examination of the evidence has become a favorite pastime amongst the people of the area. Conversations passed from generation to generation with undoubted elaboration continue to fuel debate. There are some who believe they know the identity of the killer(s) but without solid evidence, any reference here would be inappropriate.

Most however admit that the case is baffling and will forever remain unsolved.

A few interesting and sometimes conflicting tales have surfaced that can be repeated however. Some have indicated that several young women of Janie's age had acknowledged that Janie and Swinton Permenter were romantically involved and that the relationship with Earl Ray was a cover to hide this relationship from her father who disapproved of Swinton.

Another report indicates that Earl Ray had affection for Janie and kept a photograph of her in his possession till his death. This would seem to contradict his participation in such a ruse.

Some believe that the murder of Ben Walker was committed as a "murder for hire" and speculate that a man in the area known as a "dangerous individual" had committed the act for a small sum of money.

There were several reports, particularly in newspapers in other parts of the country, that the lynching of Swinton at the time of his arrest and before the first trial in Louisville was a real possibility. One paper indicated that a group of men armed with Winchester rifles had surrounded the town of Louisville and were waiting to ambush the Sheriff and his twenty deputies who were returning

Permenter from Montgomery County for trial. This paper also stated that the Governor of Mississippi had called troops to the scene to keep order.

Other papers referenced a mob of a thousand waiting at the railroad station in Louisville upon Swinton's arrival and that the sheriff and his men had difficulty making their way through the crowd to the county courthouse. It also indicated that some had declared that Swinton "must die whether or not the jury convicted him."

These reports were at best – an exaggeration and possibly completely false.

A persistent rumor of a deathbed confession by an elderly man related to the case continues to surface but no evidence of such a confession has ever been presented.

All those with firsthand information in this case have passed long ago. Without the discovery of some long lost document or signed confession, the tragic death of Miss Janie Sharp will forever remain a mystery and a subject of debate.

ABOUT THE AUTHOR

W. W. McCully is a fifth generation Mississippian with deep ties to Winston County. His work and life has taken him to many rural and historic areas across the country, sparking interest in old and often forgotten tales of rural America. He is a businessman, writer and publisher of WinstonWebNews.com. He resides on the family farm near Louisville with his wife and daughter.

W.W. McCully